AUTOBIOGRAPHY

OF

Christopher Layton

With an Account of his Funeral,
a Personal Sketch, etc., and
Genealogical Appendix

EDITED BY JOHN Q. CANNON

Salt Lake City, Utah
THE DESERET NEWS
1911

Copyright 1911
By Selina Layton Phillips
For the Layton Family Association

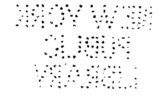

CHRISTOPHER LAYTON.
HIS LAST PORTRAIT.

PREFACE.

The inception of this little work is explained
on Page 232, where is told the selection of
committees to look up President Layton's genealogy and write a history of his life. Mrs.
Selina Layton Phillips, who was chosen secretary for this work, performed her part with
most excellent judgment and thoroughness, of
which no further evidence is required than
the delightful life story which is here presented. It has been scarcely necessary to make
any changes whatever in the narrative as prepared by her, my own part consisting in the
division of the history into chapters, with some
few additions, and a general arrangement of
the work for the printer. Acknowledgment
should also be made of the advice and active
assistance of Mrs. Mary A. Layton Swan, of
Kaysville, in supplying correct data whenever
a question arose. The full committees appointed to have the work in charge, and who
deserve the gratitude of the family for bring-

ing the volume to completion, are: Selina
Layton Phillips (secretary), Charles M. Lay-
ton, Richard G. Layton, the Arizona commit-
tee; Annie B. Jones (secretary), Christopher
Layton, Jun., Mary Ann Layton Swan, the
Utah committee.

The genealogical appendix at the end of the
book has been prepared with much care, and
as published has had final revision by Mrs.
Phillips for the Arizona, and Mrs. Swan for
the Utah, committee. Notwithstanding this,
I dare not expect that it has escaped some
errors or omissions. These, however, it is
hoped, are few, and will be viewed charitably;
for even the most critical will concede the difficulty of gathering with absolute correctness
the names and dates of so large a family, scattered over so vast an expanse of country—a
family, too, in which changes, such as births,
marriages, deaths, etc., are of almost daily occurrence. Obviously, a stopping point in the
recording of these changes had to be fixed
somewhere, and this date was fixed at July 31,
1911. It will also be noted that no record of
great-grandchildren has been attempted, lest

the scope of the appendix should run far beyond the allotted bounds.

It only remains to be said, as a last word, that this Autobiography of Christopher Layton has been prepared and published both as a tribute of affection for him and as a token of love to his posterity. It is designed to be handed down from generation to generation, to be preserved as a family memorial, to the end that in the contemplation of his busy, eventful and honorable life, the incentive to worthy deeds and righteous conduct may stand before his children and his children's children forever.

J. Q. C.

CONTENTS.

AUTOBIOGRAPHY OF

Christopher Layton.

CHAPTER I.

FROM ENGLAND TO NAUVOO.

Birth and Boyhood—Joins the Church—Marries
and Emigrates—Welcomed by the Prophet—
Patriarchal Blessings.

MY father, Samuel Layton, married Isabella Wheeler, by whom he had five children, namely, John, Bathsheba, Amos (who died in infancy), Priscilla and Christopher.

I, the youngest, was born in the small village of Thorncut, Northhill, Bedfordshire, England, on March 8, 1821.

There being no schools in our village, I had no chance for an education; and as my parents were poor, I was obliged to help in sup-

2

porting the family by working while very young. My first employment was keeping crows off the wheat fields, and I was paid thirty-six cents a week and boarded myself. This was when I was only seven years old.

I often carried my father's dinner out to him in the field, and I remember one day father tried to whip me and I ran away from him. He chased me all day but did not catch me. At night, after I had sneaked off to bed, I heard him come in and inquire of mother where I was. She said I was in bed. With fear and trembling I listened for the next remark:

"Has he had his supper?" father asked.

"No, he said he didn't want any, and seemed to be anxious to get to bed," mother answered.

Then I heard father sit down and I breathed easier as he said: "No wonder, for the young scamp ate all the apples out of my pie for my dinner and left the crusts for me." And they both laughed. Knowing that my case was settled for that time, I went to sleep.

When I was eight years old, I went to work for a Mr. Fuller on a farm. His horses were large and when I stood by them I only was as high as their shoulders, and when I put the collars and harness on them I was obliged to stand on the plow-beam to reach their backs. My main work was plowing, and here I stayed for several years.

Next I worked for a well-to-do farmer named Sargent, who lived eight miles from Bedfordshire. He employed me as a foreman on his large farm, and gave me a good salary. In this position I stayed until I joined the Church of Jesus Christ of Latter-day Saints, for which I received my discharge.

I was at this time keeping company with an excellent girl, Mary Matthews, both of us belonging to the Wesleyan Methodist church. A man named Sam Howard, who was an elder in the Latter-day Saints Church, told me that he had had a revelation that there would be four persons baptized at a meeting, and I was one of them. I laughed at the idea; but he cordially invited me to attend a meeting and I went out of curiosity mostly. When I heard the gospel I believed. Mary also attended these meetings and we went into the waters of baptism together on Jan. 1st, 1842; after which I was confirmed and ordained a priest. I worked on Mr. Coleman's large farm from this time until I came to America.

On July 10, 1842, Mary Matthews and I were married at Thorncut, Bedfordshire, England, by Rev. Taddy, and on Jan. 1st, 1843, we left Thorncut with Mr. Coleman's family, in a large baggage wagon en route for America. George Coleman and I drove the baggage in a very cumbersome wagon with three strong horses tandem. It is against the laws of England for teamsters to ride, and while both of us were riding, a policeman saw us and gave chase. We whipped up the horses and after going about three miles we outran him and slowed down again to a peaceable jog.

Leaving our wagons at Wolverhampton we went by train to Liverpool where we joined other Saints and were enrolled on the good ship "Swanton"—Capt. Davenport—as the nineteenth company of Latter-day Saint emigrants, with Lorenzo Snow as the company's captain. We stayed at Liverpool for two weeks waiting for repairs on the ship, but we

made the vessel our home, doing our cooking
and sleeping on board.

One day Brother Coleman said to me,
"Chris, ain't you going to peel some potatoes
and make us a pie?" So I went to work and
made the meat and potatoes into a pie; and
when it was baked all of the others wanted to
share with us and asked for a recipe for
"Chris's pie," as they called it.

On Jan. 16, 1843, we set sail from Liverpool
and as we slowly saw the land disappear in the
distance we sang one of the songs of Zion and
cheered each other with sympathizing words.
We were the first British emigrant company of
the season, and numbered two hundred and
twelve souls. We had a pleasant voyage across
the Atlantic, during which time just before
reaching the American shore Mary gave birth
to a little son, whom we named William M.
Layton.

After sailing for seven weeks and three days
we arrived at New Orleans and were transferred to the steamer "Amaranth" in which
we sailed up the Mississippi River. Our baby
died before we reached St. Louis, being only

about six weeks old. It was buried on shore.
We arrived at St. Louis on March 29, 1843.

We were now transferred from the steamer
to a barge, and here we had to stay two weeks
waiting for the ice to break up in the river.
My wife was sick and delicate and the weather
was raw and chilly, but we consoled ourselves
with the Lord's promises and thanked Him
that we were so near our journey's end. My
money having given out, I was obliged to bor-
row $7 of Prime Coleman.

About the 7th or 8th of April a small steamer
fastened a cable to our barge and tugged us up
the river to Nauvoo where we arrived one very
cold morning, April 12.

How rejoiced we were when we were safely
across! And there stood our Prophet on the
banks of the river to welcome us! As he
heartily grasped our hands, the fervently spok-
en words, "God bless you," sank deep into our
hearts, giving us a feeling of peace such as we
had never known before. The Saints had
congregated in front of the old post office
building to gladly welcome us to this land and
the beautiful city of Nauvoo, where the hos-

pitalities of their homes were kindly offered us. Brother Philemon C. Merrill took my wife and me home with him; his wife Cyrena gave me the first cup of milk I had in Nauvoo. Brother Merrill and Brother Sam Price were so good to us and treated me so well that I never want to forget them.

On the following day the Prophet Joseph called to see us and blessed us. After staying with Brother and Sister Merrill a few days my wife (who was still sick) and I went home with Jacob Butterfield.

The first work I did in Nauvoo was digging a well for Brother Wilson, working with Brother John Marriott, for which I received cash. I now paid Brother Coleman back the $7 I had borrowed. The Lord had truly blessed me as the Prophet had said, for I had many friends and brothers and although I had come to Nauvoo with only eight cents in my pocket I was now able to pay my debts and be a free man again, and always had work. Next I fenced in a farm for Bishop Hunter.

Brother Marriott and myself went in with some more of the brethren to build a house each, but as we thought we were not fairly dealt with and were not satisfied with the apportionment of community property, we drew out and told Joseph about it. After counseling and instructing us he gave us two and a half acres of land each and said, "You shall live to see the day when you can buy out everyone who has oppressed you." This prophecy has come true, as has all that noble man ever uttered concerning me.

We went to work at once at Big Mound and built a room 10x12 cut out of the sod. When it was pared down it looked pretty well. The first winter we had quilts for doors; we had a dirt floor and when the beds were made down, it just about filled the room. The next morning after our first night in the new house I asked Brother Marriott, "What did you dream last night?" He laughed and said, "I didn't dream anything." I continued, "I did, I dreamed you and I bought a horse," at which he laughed. "I traded my dress coat, and you your cloak." Well, we went to a man named Hamilton, who did not belong to the Church, but I told him about my dream and

showed him what we had to trade. He looked
at the clothes, and when he found that they
just fitted him he said, "Well, young men, I
don't take no stock in your dreams, but you
shan't be disappointed"—and he traded us a
nice four-year-old mare for the clothes. We
were all much pleased with the trade and we
went on our way rejoicing at our blessings.
When we showed our horse to our wives they
laughed and then cried, but we did not forget
that night to thank God for prospering and
blessing us.

Next we made a contract to do some ditch-
ing, for another horse; then we worked at cut-
ting hay and earned a wagon, and with our
horses and wagon we hauled in our wood for
winter; thus we felt that the Lord had greatly
blessed us.

Our Prophet was at this time passing
through severe trials and persecutions: his enemies sending threats to him from time to time,
but he was unruffled in his calm dignity: his
faith was so strong that he knew no fear and
at one time when he was told by his friends
that the mob was after him, he calmly replied:

"Do not be alarmed; I have no fear and shall not flee. I will find friends and the Missourians cannot slay me, I tell you in the name of Israel's God." He was subjected to thirty-eight law suits against his person and property but was never convicted. But what troubled his soul was the treachery of his friends, some of whom were very dear to him, one of his sorest afflictions being the recreancy of Sidney Rigdon, whom he had forgiven again and again but from whom he was finally obliged to solemnly withdraw the hand of fellowship in August, 1843.

His soul as well as the Saints' were filled with joy to see the growth of our beautiful city. From this country and from across the sea faithful Saints were gathering by tens and by hundreds. Homes and factories were built and the walls of the Temple were rising in grandeur, uplifting our souls with hope that soon we would be privileged to administer in the holy ordinances for our living and dead.

On Aug. 12, 1843, the revelation about the eternity and plurality of marriage was read before the High Council and Stake Presidency by Brother Hyrum, who then promised his brethren that they who accepted it should be blessed and sustained in the Church by the Spirit of God and the confidence of the Saints, and they who rejected it should fall away in their faith and power; and it was even so.

This proved to be a severe trial to many and the cause of apostasy to some, for the teaching of this revelation has been a test of personal holiness. There is not one word in it or was there one word in the Prophet's teachings other than purity and self-sacrifice. The men who have seen in this commandment a holy and exalted duty and who obeyed it in meekness and purity, have lived by their faith and have come off triumphant: while those who have sought through it to minister to evil passions have sunk and been cast out.

On Dec. 1, 1843, I received a blessing under the hands of the Patriarch Hyrum Smith, promising great things, many of which have been fulfilled. Following is a copy of this blessing:

PATRIARCHAL BLESSING

By Hyrum Smith, Patriarch, on the head of Christopher Layton, son of Samuel and Isabella Layton, born at Thorncut, England, March 8, 1821.

Brother Christopher, I lay my hands upon your head in the name of Jesus of Nazareth, to place and seal upon your head according to your lineage, your rights of priesthood, or your rights inherent; for behold, I say unto you that Priesthood when it hath power over thee in lineal descent, as also heritance, otherwise there is none inheritance, nor any power in the Priesthood, wherein the afflictions, wherein the lame, the maimed, the blind may be healed: Behold, I say unto you, Christopher, you are a descendant from the loins of Jacob, also passing through the lineage and tribe, or from the loins, of Levi: therefore you have a right to the prophetic visions, or the blessings according to the prophetic declaration, of that lineage. If you will but ask you shall receive; if you will but seek, you shall find; and if you will but knock, the mysteries of God shall be unfolded to you, and you shall be blessed in your house and habitation, in your fields and flocks, in the lineage of your posterity, in your testimony

and in your mission and calling wherein you
are called, and the day cometh when you will
stand in your place according to your appoint-
ments upon Zion, the city of the New Jeru-
salem with your posterity to enter into the possession of your inheritance and your name shall
be perpetuated with the blessings of the Priesthood in the lineage of your posterity unto the
latest generation, and your years shall be
lengthened out according to your faith. These
blessings I seal upon your head. Even so.
Amen.

Following is a copy of a letter which we
wrote to my wife's parents in England, enclos-
ing my wife's blessing:

NAUVOO, ILL., MARCH 9th, 1844.
DEAR FATHER AND MOTHER: It is with
pleasure that we write a few lines unto you,
hoping to find you well as it leaves us at this
time, and we are both living happily together,
rejoicing in the Lord and we hope you will
make yourselves happy about us. We never
wish to come to England again to live but if
we had means we would gladly cross the sea
and fetch you here, for our fathers could get
a living easier here than they can in England,
and if you will obey the gospel of Jesus Christ,
the Lord shall open a way for you to come, for

there is a great many aged people come here, older than any of you, and the Lord blesses them for so doing. The Prophet preached at the Temple on the 8th of March in the morning and one of the Twelve in the afternoon. The news was glorious; they said the Saints were thirsting after holiness and living in unity of the spirit; there never was such a cry for holiness as there is at this present time; there are a great many of them say they are willing to do whatever the Lord commands them, and the work of God is prospering all round; the Prophet is revealing glorious things, and he wishes the brethren would get the Temple on the 8th of March in the morn-receive power from on high; after they have received it they will come to England with great power, the gospel will then prove a savor of life unto life to all that believe and a savor of death to all that believe not, but we hope you will all believe it and obey.

It is customary in this country for the Saints to receive their patriarchal blessing when they get here and we have received ours and send them for you to read. The two blessings will be literally fulfilled upon us inasmuch as we are faithful and keep the commandments of God; give our love to Father and Mother Layton; we wish for them to read this letter and have a copy of the blessings, if they desire

it. We sent a letter to them three weeks ago
by post; we intend to send this by Mrs. Field-
ing, and one to Brother and Sister Martin.
Brother S—— has not the means to come at
present.

Dear Mother, I would be glad if you would
favor me in sending me word of the names of
your father and mother so that I may be baptized for them and claim them at the first resurrection, for we that come into this Church
have not only to save ourselves but our dead
friends; but if you will come in this covenant it
will cause our hearts to rejoice and yours will
rejoice when meeting those that have long slept
in the dust. I hope my dear father will not let
the world see this letter for it is only for our
friends and the Saints.

Brother Warden is not come up yet so we
have not received our parcels as yet, only those
which came in your letter, and I was much
pleased with you for your kindness. Please
to give our love to Brother and Sister Hall.
Please to send me word how they are getting
along and I hope they will obey the gospel.
Sister Shult has sent me a letter by Mr. Field-
ing,—we are living with Brother Marriott, but
our house is nearly done so that we can go in
it in a week or two. Give our love to brother
Willie and his wife, and I hope they are both
rejoicing in the Lord. Give our love to broth-

er George and his wife and I hope they will obey the gospel of Jesus Christ, otherwise they cannot inherit a celestial glory. Give our love to Brother and Sister Lee and Brother and Sister Garner and Sister Sarah Martin and T. E. Foxley. We remain your loving son and daughter,

C. AND M. LAYTON.

PATRIARCHAL BLESSING

On the head of Mary Matthews Layton, given by Hyrum Smith at Nauvoo, Ill., on Dec. 1, 1843.

Sister Mary, I lay my hands upon your head in the name of Jesus, and bless you. Behold I say unto you, Mary, you shall be blessed with prosperity, spiritually and temporally, according as you have desired, to be received in due time, as touching your house and habitation, possessions and permanent flocks and fields; nevertheless there are many trials and many perplexities in this life but in the world to come there is eternal life, a crown of immortality laid up for you. This is a promise unto you, to be a blessing and a comfort in all time to come: therefore lift up your head and be glad; behold, look and live; remember the word from the sacred article, that are precepts, and there is a blessing by promise upon your posterity and an inheritance in the lineage of your fathers, in the lineage of Abraham according to the covenants of grace, even unto fullness, to be received in fulfillment of promises obtained by Abraham, Isaac and Jacob, to be answered upon their children in this dispensation of the fullness of times, or unto their generations after them; and your blessing in all things shall be in common with your husband and your name shall be perpetuated in the line of your posterity and your years shall be multiplied as a blessing unto you. These blessings I seal upon your head. Even so. Amen.

3

CHAPTER II.

THREE BITTER YEARS—1844-'5-'6.

The Deed at Carthage—Sorrows and Persecutions —Nauvoo Evacuated — Migration Westward, "We Knew Not Where."

IN the spring of 1844 I became acquainted with some of the apostles and had many friends among the Saints, for we all loved each other and shielded and protected Joseph as much as lay in our power. One of my duties was to guard the authorities, and also to help guard the Temple.

I rented a tract of land containing forty acres, took Nealy's team of five yoke of oxen and broke the prairie and planted it in corn. It yielded a good crop, from which I realized ten cents a bushel (many selling corn that year for three or four cents a bushel). My wife made and sold bobinet lace and we prospered well.

During the months of May and June the life

of the Prophet Joseph was harassed, annoyed, and finally in the latter month taken by the mob at Carthage jail. But the work of the Church was still carried on in Nauvoo, for in May missionaries were set apart for a mission to England and the apostles were scattered over the Eastern States.

On the 16th of June Brother Joseph preached to the assembled Saints in the grove east of the Temple (while the rain fell heavily), from the revelations of St. John the Divine. After the city had been declared under martial law, the Legion was drawn up in front of the Mansion House and the Prophet, standing upon the framework of a building opposite, addressed them. He asked us if we loved him? if we would stand by him and sustain the laws of our country? And we all answered, "Yes, yes." Then he said he was content; he would die for us. "I love you, my brethren; greater love hath no man than that he lay down his life for his friends; you have stood by me in the hour of trouble, and I am willing to sacrifice my life for your preservation." Then drawing his sword—"I call God and angels to

witness that this people shall have their legal
rights or my blood shall be spilt upon the
ground * * * and my body consigned to
the tomb, but if there is one drop of blood
shed on this occasion, the sword shall never
again be sheathed until Christ comes to reign
over the earth. * * * Peace shall be tak-
en from the land which permits these crimes
against the Saints to go unavenged. * * *
May God bless you forever and ever." And
we all answered, Amen.

On the 20th of June Brother Joseph sent
word to all the apostles to return home immediately; and on the 24th he, with seventeen
others, went to Carthage.

At this time I was living at Big Mound,
an English settlement about eight miles from
Nauvoo, and there, while engaged in putting
in sod corn I heard of the Prophet's and Hyrum's death. The next morning I started to
Carthage with those who went after the
bodies. We met them on the road, Dr. Richards having dressed the wounds of John Taylor and started for Nauvoo with Joseph's and
Hyrum's bodies.

The wailing of the Saints when they saw the martyrs was terrible. Ten thousand people were addressed by Apostle Richards, who admonished them to keep the peace and trust to the law for a remedy for the awful crimes which had been committed and if the law failed, to call upon God in heaven to avenge us of our wrongs. The bodies were placed in coffins, the funeral was held, while deep grief filled our hearts and sorrow rested heavily upon us—a stricken people. The woe of the Saints cannot be described. Our Prophet and Patriarch dead, only two of the apostles with us and one of them supposed to be dying, and all this time we were in constant expectation of an attack by the mob army.

Our enemies were sure now that they had destroyed the gospel work, but it still lives, and will live, for it is the eternal work of God, and I here bear my testimony that I know that Joseph Smith, who established it, was a Prophet holy and pure.

Like sheep without a shepherd, we felt lost and bewildered, and seriously we discussed the question, "Who was highest in authority? Who

held the keys of the kingdom?" On August
6 the apostles arrived from the East, while we
were still uncertain about choosing a guardian
of the Church and it was a great relief to greet
them among us. A council of the priesthood
was called and it was not long before, with the
Twelve at the head, we felt that all things
would be managed and directed aright. In
the person of the President of the Twelve,
Brigham Young, we knew that a great character had arisen, to build upon the foundation
laid by Joseph Smith, a kingdom whose equal
"there never was in the world." Now feeling at
peace, we pursued our usual work: the work
on the Temple was pushed forward as rapidly
as possible.

On August 17, 1844, a little daughter was
born to us, at Nauvoo, and we named her
Elizabeth M.

In the fall of 1844 I moved to La Harpe, Ill.
John Marriott and I worked for Mr. White,
and in the spring of '45, we rented the farm
of him and put in a crop of corn, and had a
good yield. Brother Coleman's boys came to
La Harpe and worked, taking grain for pay

and we stored their grain on our place. After harvest we returned to Big Mound.

Four of us took up one hundred and sixty acres of land and divided it between us; I built a house on my forty acres—one mile from the Mound. An old lady was living on one corner of my forty, and she was taken sick with typhoid fever. It seemed too bad for her to be there all alone and I asked my wife to go and take care of her. She said she had thought about it, but did not know how I would get along with the cooking work, etc.; but I told her to go, I'd get along all right. So she went, but the lady soon died, and then Mary was taken down with the same fever. I moved her to Sam Payne's house where she could have better care, but in Sept., 1845, she quietly passed away from us. I walked three miles but could get no lumber and was obliged to take a log, and I helped to hew a coffin out of that, then I carried it back on my shoulders, then, with three teams, we went to Nauvoo and buried her. Thus I was left alone with my little girl of thirteen months.

Among my neighbors were two good friends,

Wm. B. Smith and his excellent wife, who had no children, and they took my baby and cared for her as tenderly as they could have done for their own; they learned to love her so dearly and she became so attached to them that they could not give her up and she remanied in their family until she was married in 1861.*

In January, 1845, the legislature, yielding to popular clamor, repealed the charter of the city of Nauvoo. We now had no protection whatever.

In the spring of 1845 I was ordained an Elder.

On April 8, 1845, Brigham Young received a letter of advice from Gov. Ford of Illinois, saying we had better get off by ourselves, where we might enjoy peace, and counseling

---

*On April 11, 1861, Elizabeth M. Layton married William W. Galbraith at Kaysville, Utah, by whom she had six children, five boys and one girl; two boys are dead. In 1889 they moved to Mexico, where she still resides. In April, 1897, W. W. Galbraith was taken sick and after lingering nine months he passed away on Jan. 1st, 1898. He died in full faith in the gospel, exhorting all the family to be true to it; leaving four wives and twenty-three living children to mourn the loss of a kind husband and loving father.

him to take us "out to California." This was
unnecessary as we were already making preparations to carry into effect the plan which the
Prophet Joseph had given of finding a place
of refuge in the West beyond the Rockies.

In May a faint effort was made to bring
the murderers of Joseph and Hyrum to justice,
but after a trial they were "honorably acquit-
ted," which news made the mob element so
bold that they committed fresh outrages.
Houses were burned and people driven from
place to place, till, fearing massacre, the Saints
living in the settlements came into Nauvoo for
protection. On May 24 the walls of the Temple
were finished, Brigham laying the last stone
in the presence of the assembled Saints, and
pronouncing a benediction; the Saints shouting
"Hosanna to God and the Lamb, Amen and
Amen."

After my wife's death in September I went
to see about the grain I had left stored at
La Harpe, and while there a mob broke out.
I was riding a fine mare noted for her racing
qualities and I started back toward Nauvoo.
Some of the mobbers seeing me came after

me, but I encouraged my mare to try her speed and we soon left them far behind.

On October 5 the first meeting was held in the Temple; the apostles administering in the holy ordinances to hundreds of people, continuing day and night; and by the end of December, over a thousand had received these ordinances; all this was done while we were making preparations to leave the city. These were busy and sad times. Hundreds were making tents and wagon covers and packing preparatory to leaving their homes; companies were organized and numbered, each with its wagon shop, wheelwrights, carpenters, etc., and all busily employed. It was intended that each family of 5 persons should have 1 good wagon, 3 yoke of cattle, 2 cows, 3 sheep, 1,000 lbs. of flour, 20 lbs. sugar, 1 rifle and ammunition, a tent and poles, from 10 to 20 lbs. of seeds, 25 to 100 lbs. farming tools, bedding and cooking utensils. But many a family were driven out with almost nothing.

I came out from Nauvoo with the first company of exiles, my team pulling the little cannon called the "Old Sow." We crossed the

Mississippi River on the ice on February 6,
1846.

> "We've left the City of Nauvoo,
> And our beloved Temple, too;
> And to the wilderness we go,
> Amid the winter frosts and snow."
> —*Eliza Snow.*

That night we camped in the snow, sleeping in our wagons, and before morning there
were nine new babies in our camp.

On the 7th Brother Brigham organized the
camp in order for traveling. All of the exiles
pushed on to Sugar Creek, nine miles into
Iowa, and from there a new start was taken,
the advance companies having waited until all
had arrived. It was bitterly cold, and much
suffering had been endured. Now the labor
of temporary organization began. Getting into a wagon, Brother Brigham said in a voice
clear and distinct: "Attention, the whole camp
of Israel!" Then he gave us plain practical
instructions as to the order and arrangement
of the camp; with a tone of authority, tempered with love and firmness, he told us: "We
will have no laws we cannot keep, but we will
have order in the camp. If any want to live

in peace when we have left this place, they must toe the mark."

Our orders were to advance on the 1st of March, and about noon on that day we broke encampment and soon nearly four hundred wagons were moving to—we knew not where.

While here, Sister Eliza R. Snow composed two poems applicable to the occasion, one of which is given below:

CAMP OF ISRAEL.
No. 2.

Lo, a mighty host of Jacob,
  Tented on the western shore
Of the noble Mississippi,
  They had crossed, to cross no more.
At the last day-dawn of winter,
  Bound with frost and wrapped in snow;
Hark! the cry is "Onward, onward!
  Camp of Israel, rise and go."

All at once is life and motion—
  Trunks, and beds, and baggage fly;
Oxen yoked, and horses harnessed,
  Tents rolled up and passing by:
Soon the carriage wheels are moving,
  Onward to a woodland dell,
Where at sunset all are quartered—
  Camp of Israel, all is well.

Thickly 'round the tents are clustered,
  Neighb'ring smokes together blend;
Supper served, the hymns are chanted,
  And the evening prayers ascend.
Last of all the guards are stationed—
  Heavens! must guards be serving here?
Who would harm the houseless exiles?
  Camp of Israel, never fear.

Where is Freedom? Where is Justice?
  Both have from this nation fled;
And the blood of martyred Prophets
  Must be answered on its head!
Therefore, to your tents, O Jacob!
  Like our father Abra'm dwell;
God will execute His purpose—
  Camp of Israel, all is well.

We moved slowly onward only making five
miles the first day, and thus the weary march
was slowly continued from day to day in mud,
snow and rain; but sustained by Divine power,
we pressed on in search of a new home. I
traveled with the Presidency. We were often
delayed by freshets, one time having to wait
for three weeks to cross Shoal Creek near the
Chariton River.

We made a halt at last at a place which we

named Garden Grove and built some log huts
and planted corn, some remaining to cultivate the same and prepare a resting place for
.the weary Saints who should follow us, while
the main body of the camp moved on to another
halting place. Because I remained at Garden
Grove some of the men wanted to take my
team to move the Saints, but Brother Brigham
said: "No; this man has cut brush to keep
us warm, while you were warming yourselves
at the fire he made and you can't have his
team."

On again till we reached a place which
Apostle Parley Pratt had named Mt. Pisgah,
and here we made another station for those
who should follow. All hands went to work,
some breaking sod, dragging down and getting land in order, while others,—I among
them—split rails and fenced in the big field
all ready for planting. This was all done in
one day, and at night we had singing, a dance,
and then each family had their prayers and we
slept peacefully, and safe in our Heavenly
Father's care.

CHAPTER III.

THE GOVERNMENT'S CALL.

Five Hundred Men Asked For—Mustering and
Marching—Brave Looks but Sore Hearts—
Brigham Young's Promise.

ABOUT June 15, 1846, Brigham Young,
with the vanguard of the migrating
trains, reached the Missouri River, followed
by the main body in July. We stopped at a
place on the east side of the river, which we
named Kanesville, but it is now known as
Council Bluffs. The Pottawatomie and Oma-
ha Indians were very friendly and later in the
season, in what is now called Florence, Neb.,
we founded the celebrated Winter Quarters,
with a population of about four thousand souls.

It was the intention of our leader to hasten
onward that summer and fall with a band of
pioneers to explore the Rocky Mountains. "The
muster for volunteers, for this purpose, was in
progress at Mount Pisgah, under the direction

of Apostle Woodruff who had recently returned from England, when the Mormon nation of twelve thousand souls, stretching across
the whole of Iowa, was startled by a call for
volunteers—for a Mormon Battalion—to do
battle for their country against Mexico. This
event changed the plans, and the Saints were
compelled to remain in Winter Quarters, and
in the other settlements in Iowa, over winter."*

Great was the consternation in camp at
Mount Pisgah, when on June 26, 1846, it was
told among us that a United States officer had
called for volunteers, and naturally we thought
it was only another threat being carried out.

That there may be a better understanding
of the call from the United States I will quote
from the "Life of Brigham Young," showing
how it originated:

"About the time that the Saints left Nauvoo, Elder Samuel Brannan sailed with two
hundred and thirty-five Mormons, on the ship
'Brooklyn' for California, intending to join
those who left Nauvoo somewhere on the Pacific Coast. Before sailing from New York,

*Life of Brigham Young.

Brannan entered into a peculiar agreement with one A. G. Benson, who represented a company of Washington sharpers, requiring the Mormons to transfer to said Benson and Co. the odd numbers of all the lands and town lots which they might acquire in the country where they should settle. * * * Brannan was prevailed upon to sign such an agreement and he forwarded it to the Mormon leaders for their approval and signatures, with the information that if they did not sign the document President Polk would issue a proclamation setting forth that it was the intention of the Mormons to take sides with either Mexico or Great Britain, which latter country then claimed Oregon, in the impending struggle against the United States; intercept them, and order them to be disarmed and dispersed; but if they did sign, then they were to be allowed to proceed unmolested. When this strange document came to President Young, he called a council of the Twelve, (Sugar Creek, Feb. 17, 1846), resulting in the emphatic rejection of the proposition without a reply. 'We concluded that our trust is in God, and we look to Him for protection,' said they, and, added President Young, 'This is a plan of political demagogues to rob the Latter-day Saints of millions and compel them to submit to it by threats of Federal bayonets.'

4

"The appearance of Captain J. Allen in
Mount Pisgah, however, was not due to the
Brannan letter but resulted from a different
cause. * * * Shortly after the Saints left
Nauvoo, Brigham Young had sent Elder Jesse
C. Little to Washington to try to obtain aid, if
possible, from the nation, to assist them in their
march. It was thought that they might be
permitted to freight government provisions
and stores to Oregon and other Pacific Coast
points. Elder Little succeeded to such an extent that assistance was about to be granted,
when the breaking out of the war with Mexico determined President Polk upon the de-
sign of hurriedly taking possession of California, and of using the migrating Mormons
for this purpose. This project was matured
and about to be carried out, when it was
changed through the influence of Senator
Thomas Benton, an old enemy of the Mormons—a Missourian. Another plan was then
adopted, which involved a call for five hundred
Mormon volunteers to form a part of the force
which was to invade New Mexico and California, under Gen. Kearney, the commander of
the army of the West, then at Santa Fe. When
the commander received the President's order,
he detailed Captain Allen to proceed to the
camps of the Saints, muster the battalion, and
march them to Fort Leavenworth there to be

armed and prepared for service, then to follow the trail of Gen. Kearney and the main
army.

"To this day there is a difference of opin-
ion as to whether it was meant for the good or
destruction of the Mormons. The Saints in
that day viewed it in the latter light. The
leaders looked upon it as a test of loyalty of
the Mormons to their country, and so, when
the recruiting officer came to Brigham Young
at Council Bluffs,   *   *   *   he promptly replied: 'You shall have your Battalion, Captain Allen, and if there are not young men
enough, we will take the old men, and if they
are not enough, we will take the women.'   *
*   *   *   Men were sent to all the camps to
summon to headquarters the old men and the
boys to supply the place of the men—the
strength of the people—who were enlisted in
the Battalion. Taking up the keynote from
the leader, 'You shall have your Battalion,'
leading elders cheerfully responded to the call."

Others fell into line, for had not our leader
said:

"We must raise this Battalion. It is right;
and who cares for sacrificing our comfort for
a few years? I say unto you, magnify the
laws. There is no law in the United States,

or in the Constitution, but I am ready to make honorable."

Col. Thomas L. Kane, who was present at the time of the muster, says: "A central mass meeting for council, an American flag brought out from the storehouse of things rescued and hoisted to the top of a tree mast, and in three days the force was reported, mustered, organized and ready to march."

One circumstance I well remember: some of the women, feeling sure that they would never see their husbands again, said they would never live to be a soldier's widow, and one lady remarked, "I would rather be a soldier's widow than a coward's wife;" and that was the feeling that our brave women had when they had to part with their loved ones; each one being brave for another's sake.

Our noble leaders, though anxious and trouble-worn, seemed desirous of throwing off the burden of heavy and sorrowful thoughts, and on our last afternoon together we had a farewell ball in the bowery, they leading off in the dance. At sunset we had a song and an elder asked the blessings of heaven on all who,

with purity of heart and brotherhood of spirit, had mingled in this society, and we all went
to our camps.

The parting cannot be described which took
place on the 16th of July, 1846. As we were
marching past Sister Smith's camp, she held
up my little girl to see me and she shook her
hand and said, "by-by." My heart was full
and I waved my hand and marched on, leaving behind me all I had on earth—my baby
daughter. But she was in good hands, while
many were leaving wives and little ones with
scant food and clothing—we could only com-
mit them all to our kind Heavenly Father's
care and protection.

President Young had encouraged us by saying that our families should be well cared for,
at least fare as well as he did, and that he
would see that they were helped along. He
also said that not one of those that had enlisted would fall by the nation's foe, that our
only fighting would be with wild beasts; that
there would not be as many bullets whistle
around our ears as did around Dr. Willard
Richards' in Carthage jail; and improbable as

it naturally looked at the time and during our travels, still these predictions were literally fulfilled.

We were marched to the Missouri River, a distance of eight miles, to purchase blankets and other necessary articles for the campaign; and here on the 18th of July, Elders Young, Kimball, P. P. Pratt, Richards, Taylor and Woodruff met in council with the officers and gave us our last charge and blessing, with a firm promise that "on condition of faithfulness on our part, our lives should be spared, our expedition should result in good and our names should be held in honorable remembrance to all generations. We must remember our prayers, always revere the name of Deity, and virtue and cleanliness must be strictly observed; treat all men with kindness; never take that which did not belong to us, even from our worst enemies; always treat all prisoners with kindness and never take life when it could be avoided."

Captain Allen, our commander, was a brave, manly officer with pleasing, kindly manners and soon gained the good-will of our people as well as their love.

CHAPTER IV.

THE MORMON BATTALION.

From the Bluffs to Leavenworth—Death of Col. Allen—Weary March Westward—An Inhuman Surgeon—Arrival at Santa Fe.

I JOINED the Mormon Battalion of Iowa Volunteers, Company C, Infantry, as a private, my number being 47. The officers of Company C were: James Brown, Captain; George W. Rosecrans, First Lieutenant;. Samuel Thompson, Second Lieutenant; Robert Clift, Third Lieutenant.

There also accompanied us several families of the soldiers, the women acting as laundresses for the companies; also some boys who were too young for soldiers and served as servants to officers, and deserve much praise for their youthful patriotism and bravery.

Previous to taking up our line of march, on the 20th of July, the men of each company subscribed liberally of their wages to be sent back for the support of their families and to aid in gathering the poor from Nauvoo.

The next day we had a rainstorm and we traveled about four miles in the mud. Elder Jesse C. Little spent the night with us and the next day, at the request of the officers, he delivered a short and encouraging address to the command while formed in a hollow square.

On the morning of the 23rd we had to perform the painful duty of burying Brother Samuel Boley. This was the first death in the ranks. He was wrapped in his blanket and buried in a rough lumber coffin, which was the best we could get. Next day we crossed the Nishnabotany River and camped near Lincoln, Mo. Several parties were taken sick but were healed by using consecrated oil and laying on of hands, and we all went on our way rejoicing.

On the 25th, the command being out of flour, some of us went to bed fasting, while others made supper on parched corn. No flour was obtained for two days, during which time we traveled in the heat and dust for thirty-eight miles, and many of us sick from our long forced marches. When we had crossed the Nodaway River and camped at Oregon, Mo., a man who had a load of flour for us stopped outside of camp and refused to deliver it to the quartermaster because he was a Mormon, saying he would deliver to no one but the Colonel. That noble officer, however, was highly insulted, and ordered him to bring that flour into camp and deliver it immediately or be put under arrest and guard. "Good for the Colonel!" and "God bless the Colonel!" were repeated from one end of the camp to the other. Passing through this country we saw many of the old mobocrats who regretted that they had persecuted the Saints. They would be glad to have their Mormon neighbors back again; were dumbfounded to see the Battalion march with so much order and civility.

On the 29th we marched through St. Joseph, to the tune of "The Girl I Left Behind Me;" on the 30th, through Bloomington; on the 31st. the thriving town of Weston was reached, then to the ferry opposite Fort Leavenworth. Here we were five hours crossing and making our way to the garrison. We camped on the public square of the fort, and our tents were given to us, which added much to our comfort, and

the merry songs which sounded through the
camp made all feel like "casting dull care
away."

The distance from Council Bluffs to Fort
Leavenworth is in round numbers two hundred
miles directly down the Missouri River. On
the day of our arrival in garrison we received
orders that Dr. George B. Sanderson was appointed surgeon to serve the Mormon Battalion, and would have medical supplies for our
trip to California.

On the 3rd of August, Companies A, B and
C drew our arms which consisted of United
States flintlock musket (with bayonet), twenty-
four cartridges, belt and cartouches; we also
drew a haversack, a knapsack, a blanket (carried on top of knapsack) and provisions. Col.
Allen accompanied the officer who issued the
arms, and seeing us around the door, each one
anxious to receive the first gun, said, in his
good-natured, humorous way: "Stand back,
boys; don't be in a hurry to get your muskets; you will want to throw the d——d things
away before you get to California."

On the 5th we drew forty-two dollars each,

as clothing money for the year; the most of
which we sent back by Elder P. P. Pratt for
the support of our families and for gathering
the poor from Nauvoo. (I often think and
wonder if people nowadays would do it?)

Colonel Allen was heard to say, while talking to an officer of the garrison, that he "had
not been under the necessity of giving the
word of command to the Mormons the second time. The men, though unacquainted
with military tactics, were willing to obey orders." Volunteers from different parts of the
country came into the garrison every day to
get their outfits; some of them were rough,
desperate characters, and quarreling and fighting was not unusual among them. The first
Sunday spent by us in Fort Leavenworth was
observed by holding service. Elder Geo. P.
Dykes preached a kind of military and gospel sermon.

The weather here was very warm and we
had many cases of sickness, from ague. Colonel Allen was taken seriously ill after our
arrival at Fort Leavenworth and he instructed
the senior Captain, Jefferson Hunt, to advance

with the command while he would remain to recruit and complete the business pertaining to the outfitting of the Battalion. On August 12, 1846, Companies A, B and C took up the line of march for Santa Fe, and traveled that day five miles, finding only poor water and little of it, which made it bad for the sick, several of whom had raging fevers. On the 15th we crossed the Kansas or Kaw River, which at the ferry was about three hundred yards wide, and we were ferried over by Shawnee Indians. In the evening we reached Spring Creek and found more than a dozen springs within twenty yards of each other. Here we stayed for two days and all got soaked through by a rain storm; it also hailed and the wind blew terribly. We moved on to Stone Coal Creek—about four miles—where we were overtaken by the others, Companies D and E, and found Colonel Sterling Price and his command of cavalry, who had left the garrison two days ahead of us, encamped. We rested to dry our clothes and in the afternoon the Battalion was called together and addressed by Captain Hunt, Corporal Tyler, Brother Han-

cock, and Sergeant Hyde respectively. An
excellent spirit prevailed and all seemed to appreciate the remarks. Three persons were
baptized for their health and one for the re-
mission of sins.

On the 21st Adjutant Dykes arrived from
the garrison and brought word that Colonel
Allen was still very sick. Many prayers were
offered for his recovery for he was beloved by
the command. On the 22nd we were again
moving but had traveled only a short distance when we came to a small stream which
was very hard to cross. Long ropes were
fastened to the wagons on each side, with ten
or fifteen men to each rope to aid the teams,
and it was noon before we were all over, then
on over a fine prairie of rich bottom land—
our sick seemed much improved. Next day
we passed remnants of an old stone wall, five
feet thick, and other ruins of some ancient
city; then over beautiful rich lands that would
make good farms. On the 25th we met a
gentleman returning from Bent's Fort, and we
sent letters back to anxious friends. On the
26th, while crossing a creek where the water

was very deep and the banks high, one of our company's wagons turned over, upsetting six or seven men and several women. The men on the banks jumped in and pulled them all out, but they all had a good wetting.

On the 27th we received the sorrowful news of the death of Colonel Allen, which had occurred on August 23, 1846, and on the 29th Adjutant Dykes preached his funeral sermon with some very appropriate remarks by Captain Hunt. After receiving the news of the death of Colonel Allen, our officers held a council and agreed that Captain Hunt should assume the command of the Battalion, which was unanimously sustained by the men. We then continued our march under his orders to Council Grove, where Lieutenant Smith, Major Walker, and Dr. Geo. B. Sanderson came to us, bringing a letter to Captain Hunt from Major Horton, of Fort Leavenworth, informing him that the government property in possession of the Battalion was not receipted for and advising us to submit to the command of Lieutenant Smith, and he would send the receipts to us for the same, as it might save us considerable trouble. When the command was given to Lieutenant Smith, the soldiers were not consulted and we all felt that it was Captain Hunt's right to command, so when it was known that Lieutenant Smith was our commander, even before his character was known to us, it caused a greater gloom throughout the Battalion than the death of Colonel Allen had.

On the morning of the 31st of August we marched to Diamond Springs under the new commander, and were mustered and inspected by him; next day on to Lost Springs, being a lonesome place, with no trees, and we followed the Arab style of digging narrow trenches in which we burned weeds to heat water for our tea and coffee; our food we had cooked the previous day. On the 2nd of September we camped at Cottonwood Creek in the Comanche country, and these Indians were hostile at this time. Lieutenant Smith here pulled several of our sick men out of the wagons with horrid oaths and threats because they had neglected to report themselves to Dr. Sanderson. Our instructions from Brother Brigham had been, "If you are sick, live by faith, and let surgeon's medicine alone if you want to live, using only such herbs and mild food as are at your disposal. If you heed this counsel you will prosper;" but Lieutenant Smith and Dr. Sanderson compelled us to take their drugs out of an old iron spoon, which he considered "good enough for the Mormons." After this it was customary every morning for the sick (many of the Battalion having chills and fever) to be marched to the tune of "Jim along Joe" to the doctor's quarters, and take their portion of calomel and arsenic, or decoction of bayberry bark and camomile flowers. So determined was Dr. Sanderson that we should take his medicine that he threatened with an oath to cut the throat of any one who gave anything without his orders. Those who were unable to march to sick call reported themselves and received not only medicine but cursing. It would be difficult to find American citizens from any other community who would have submitted to the tyranny and abuse that the Battalion did from Smith and Sanderson. Nor would we have done so on any consideration other than as servants to our God and patriots to our country.

On the 5th of September we saw a few buffalo and the next day plenty of them. One
of the soldiers killed one and we thought the
meat pretty good eating though it was a little tough. On the 7th we were ordered on
parade and had the military law read to us
for the first time, in order that we might be
better posted in regard to campaign duties. On
the 9th we camped at Pawnee Fork, which
stream was very difficult to cross, and occupied a long time; each wagon had to be let
down the bank with ropes, while on the opposite bank from twenty to thirty men with
ropes helped the teams in pulling the wagons
up. The water was very muddy like the Missouri.

The next day we had a heavy rain storm
and found no timber to cook our supper with.
We met an express from Santa Fe who told
us of the surrender of that place to General
S. F. Kearney, and gave us an order from that
general directing the Battalion to leave the
road and not go by way of Bent's Fort, but to
march direct to Santa Fe, which of course we
proceeded to do, although the most of our

6

provisions and two pieces of artillery were in
advance of us toward the Fort.

About noon on the 11th we reached the Arkansas River. At this point it was about a
quarter of a mile wide and filled with sand,
with here and there a small stream of brackish
water; we dug holes about two or three feet
deep in the sand and obtained enough water
for our needs. The afternoon was spent in
a general washing, and many fish were caught
by spearing them in the shallow water with
swords and bayonets. The supper that night
was thankfully received as a great treat. After
crossing the river we overtook five companies
óf Colonel Sterling Price's regiment from
western Missouri whom we found to be a profane, wicked ànd vulgar set of men. We were
not rejoiced to see Colonel Price, as we knew
him in days of old as a commander of the mob
militia in Far West in 1838.

At this time Captain Higgins of Company
D with a guard of ten men was detailed to
take a number of the families that accompanied the Battalion to Pueblo to winter, and
many of us were dissatisfied with this move,

as Brigham Young had counseled the officers
not to allow the Battalion to be separated on
any account.   Lieutenants Pace and Gully opposed it and requested a council and wished
to send letters to the Twelve Apostles; but
Adjutant Dykes objected to this, saying there
was no time for councils, and President Young
did not know our circumstances.   The families, therefore, were forced to leave us on
the 16th of September, and take up their line
of march to Pueblo.   While here Brother Alva
Phelps died, a victim of Dr. Sanderson's
strong medicine.*   He was buried on the south
side of the Arkansas River.   That evening we
noticed what appeared to be a star in the
eastern sky dancing in the air.   It moved both
up and down, and north and south, directly in

---

*"It is understood that he begged Dr. Sander-
son not to give him any medicine, as he needed
only a little rest, and then would return to duty;
but the doctor prepared his dose and ordered him
to take it, which he declined doing, whereupon the
doctor, with some horrid oaths, forced it down
him with an old, rusty spoon.   A few hours later
he died, and the general feeling was that the doctor had killed him."—Mormon Battalion History.

the course we had traveled, and finally sunk out of sight.

The next day we marched twenty-five miles across a dreary desert and suffered intensely from the great heat and want of water. Our teams also suffered much, and then the mirage was such an aggravation—it had the appearance of fog rising from water and then would look like a lake of clear water, but it went on ahead of us and stopped when we did. We passed one pond full of insects of all sizes and shapes, out of which we drove several thousand buffaloes. No luxury was ever more thankfully received. The few whose canteens were not exhausted of course did not use it, but bad as it was, it was welcome to most of us. We put the water in a vessel and then sucked it through a silk handkerchief. The next day we continued on across the dry, parched desert without finding any water, except a pond similar to the one the day before, which was hailed with great joy and considered a great blessing. Again we made a "dry camp" but started at 4 o'clock in the morning and traveled ten miles before breakfast.

It does not appear whether Colonel Smith had had no experience in traveling with teams, or whether he desired to use up the teams and leave the Battalion on the plains helpless; but for the last hundred miles, where there had been but little feed, he had shown no wisdom or care in preserving either man or beast; but on the contrary, no matter whether our drives were to be long or short, he had driven on forced marches, on which account many had failed very fast. Our only fuel for the last ten days had been nothing but buffalo "chips" and sometimes these were very scarce.

On the night of the 20th, having traveled ten miles, we camped before the sink of the Cimmaron Creek, where we obtained brackish water by digging holes in the sand. On the 21st we marched eighteen miles and again camped on the Cimmaron and had to dig in sand again for water. It looked as if the Colonel and surgeon were determined to kill us, first by forced marches to make us sick, then compel us to take calomel or to walk and do duty. Our officers held a council with our spiritual advisers, David Pettigrew and Levi W.

Hancock, in which our condition was discussed to see if anything could be done to ameliorate it. Then they appealed to the Colonel, trying to reason with him, pointing out the fact of the men and beasts failing because of these forced marches—that many of the men were badly salivated from the malpractice of Dr. Sanderson, etc., but he merely replied to the effect that he could do nothing, and the subject had to be dropped.

On the 25th we marched twenty miles over a rough and mountainous road and camped at Gold Springs where we found good water and some little timber. On the 26th we saw many deer, elk, and antelope; reached Cedar Springs, saw cedar, spruce and cottonwood. On the 27th shot a few antelope which added to our scanty rations was a real treat. We now could see numerous mountain peaks, the first that many of us had ever seen, and during the next day our way was over hills and high ridges; now wild turkey and bear were added to our camp supper.

On the 30th we passed Rock Creek, but men and teams were failing, and as we found no

feed for animals we traveled till 9 o'clock at
night and were on the move again at daylight.
About noon we passed near the walls of an
ancient structure, which might have been a
castle or fortification, and numerous canals,
which evidently had not been used for generations. On October 2 we reached Red River
and on the 3rd a council was called in which
the commander said he had received orders
from General Kearney that unless the command reached Santa Fe by the 10th we would
be discharged. Therefore he suggested that
we select fifty able-bodied men from each
company to take the best teams and travel on a
double forced march, leaving the sick with the
weak teams to follow as they could. Quite a
number opposed this because they did not
wish to divide us, but it was carried, and the
Battalion was accordingly divided, all the able-
bodied soldiers, most of the commissioned officers, Colonel Smith and Dr. Sanderson, making
their way with all possible haste to Santa Fe.
After the division, those who were left at the
rear, not being now obliged to take medicine,
and the feed and water being better, were get-

ting stronger each day, and they spent no unnecessary time on the road.

The first division arrived at Santa Fe on the
evening of October 9, 1846, and the second
division three days later.

On our approach General Doniphan, the
commander of the post, ordered a salute of a
hundred guns to be fired in honor of the Mormon Battalion. This same general was much
pleased to find a number of old friends and
acquaintances among the soldiers, whom he
knew to be honorable, upright and loyal men,
and it was probably the memory of the wrongs
which they had suffered from the Missouri
mobocrats which prevented him from extending any courtesies to Colonel Sterling Price
and his disgraceful cavalry command on their
arrival.*

---

*"When Col. Sterling Price, with his cavalry
command, which left Fort Leavenworth two or
three days ahead of us, arrived at Santa Fe, he
was received without any public demonstration,
and when he learned of the salute which had been
fired in honor of the 'Mormons,' he was greatly
chagrined and enraged."—Mormon Battalion History.

CHAPTER V.

SANTA FE TO TUCSON.

Col. Cooke in Command—A Story of Starvation
and Toil—Prayers Answered—Battle with Bulls
on San Pedro—Soldier Poetry.

COLONEL P. St. George Cooke who was
awaiting us in Santa Fe took command on
October 13, 1846. He instructed Captain Jas.
Brown to. take command of men who, from
sickness, had been reported as incapable of
making the journey to California, also the
laundresses, who would suffer much on such a
march and would be an incumbrance to the
expedition, and march them to Fort Pueblo to
winter. Twenty-four of this detachment were
from Company C and they left us on the 18th
of October.

By special arrangement and consent, the Battalion was paid in checks—not very available
at Santa Fe.* On the 19th we took leave of

*Colonel Cooke's diary.

John D. Lee, Lieutenant Gully and others who
started with our checks for Council Bluffs, and
as soon as they left we broke camp and traveled six miles to "Aqua Frio," (cold water)
the nearest point for grazing. We were supplied with rations for sixty days; full rations
of flour, sugar, coffee and salt; salt pork only
for thirty days and soap for twenty. We started
with mules, ox teams, wagons and pack sad-
dles; these mules and oxen, with a few excep-
tions were the same ones (worn-out and brok-
en down) that we had driven all the way from
Council Bluffs, and some of them had been
driven all the way from Nauvoo.

After we had traveled past every place
where it would be possible to purchase provisions for a time, to the surprise of the command the rations were reduced by the following:

Orders No. 11.
HEADQUARTERS MORMON BATTALION,
SANTA FE.
Until further orders, three-fourths pound
flour, also three-fourths rations sugar and cof-
fee, will be issued. Beef, one and a half

pounds, will be issued for a day's ration. *
* * * Commanders of companies will be
held strictly responsible that the issue of rations is made carefully as now ordered. The
welfare and safety of the Battalion may de-
pend on it.

(2). Hereafter, no muskets or knapsacks
will be carried in a public wagon or on a public
mule without orders, or express permission of
the commanding officer, and no one will leave
his company a quarter of a mile without permission, and no musket will be fired in camp.
The officer of the day will attend to the execu-
tion of these regulations and confine under
guard any one who disobeys them. At reveille
all will turn out under arms. The company
commanders will order turns of guard or confine those who fail. After roll call the ranks
will be opened and an officer will pass down
each rank and see that all are fully armed and
equipped. Immediately after roll call, breakfast will be disposed of and everything packed
in the wagons. * * * * All this will be
done without waiting for signals or the loss of
a moment. The teams will be hitched up as
the teamsters get their breakfast. * * * *
Every teamster must have one or more buckets,
or camp kettles with which to water his team.
The teams will not stop to water unless ordered by the commanding officer, as everything

depends on our animals. I call all the officers and the quartermaster sergeants of companies and the teamsters and assistants to do the best for them possible. The order will be read twice at the head of each company by its commander.

By order of

LIEUT. COL. COOKE,

(Signed)   G. P. DYKES, Adjutant.

This order was strictly observed. The first breach of regulations was by an officer, Captain Hunter of Company C, who had remained in Santa Fe without the consent of the commanding officer, and was promptly punished. Thus we found out that our new commander, although very strict, was impartial; he believed that the officers should obey first, and set the example to the men.

On October 23 the quartermaster exchanged thirty of our worthless mules for half that number of fresh ones; the Colonel also purchased eight and obtained ten yoke of oxen. Two of our poorest heavy wagons were also exchanged for lighter and better ones. The hand of the Lord was thus manifested to us, for without something of the kind, we must have been left without conveyance in the desert.

On the 25th Sergeant E. Elmer of Company C was reduced to the ranks for neglecting to form his company while reveille was beating, and for telling his Colonel that he did so because he could not see to call the roll; but he was subsequently restored to his office and retained the respect and friendship of all of us.

While marching down the Rio Del Norte we found the roads extremely sandy in many places and the men, though carrying blankets, knapsacks, cartridge boxes and muskets on their backs and living on short rations, had to pull at long ropes to aid the teams. We were ready to eat anything that would furnish any nourishment—the rations issued to us did not satisfy the cravings of hunger. When one of the fat cattle was slaughtered for beef the Colonel gave positive orders that no more of them should be killed as we needed them for work; only those that were unable to work from sheer exhaustion and weakness, could be used for beef, and from that time the carcasses were issued as rations. Nothing was wasted that could possibly be utilized for food: even the hides, tripe and entrails, all were eagerly devoured, sometimes without even water to wash it down. The marrow bones were considered a luxury, and rich indeed would be the dinner of the mess whose turn it was to receive them.

On the 27th we had a cold rain in the valley of the Rio Del Norte, and heavy snow fell in the mountains, but the storm settled the sandy roads, making them easier to travel.

Our cheerful camp singer, Levi W. Hancock, ofttimes amused and entertained us while around our camp fires—and often composed songs to fit the occasion as the following will show:

THE DESERT ROUTE.

While here, beneath a sultry sky,
Our famished mules and cattle die;
Scarce aught but skin and bones remain
To feed poor soldiers on the plain.

Chorus:
How hard, to starve and wear us out
Upon this sandy, desert route.

We sometimes now for lack of bread,
Are less than quarter rations fed.
And soon expect, for all of meat
Naught else than broke-down mules to eat.

Now, half-starved oxen, over-drilled,
'Too weak to draw, for beef are killed;
And gnawing hunger prompting men
To eat small entrails and the skin.

Sometimes we quarter for the day,
While men are sent ten miles away,
On our back track, to place in store
An ox, give out the day before.

And when an ox is like to die,
The whole camp halts, and we lay by;
The greedy wolves and buzzards stay,
Expecting rations for the day.

Our hardships reach their rough extremes
When valiant men are roped with teams,
Hour after hour, and day by day,
To wear our strength and lives away.

The teams can hardly drag their loads
Along the hilly, sandy roads,
While trav'ling near the Rio Grande
O'er hills and dales of heated sand.

We see some twenty men, or more,
With empty stomachs, and foot-sore,
Bound to one wagon, plodding on
Through sand, beneath a burning sun.

A doctor which the government
Has furnished proves a punishment!
At his rude call of "Jim along Joe,"
The sick and halt to him must go.

Both night and morn, this call is heard;
Our indignation then is stirr'd,
And we sincerely wish in hell
His arsenic and calomel.

To take it, if we're not inclined,
We're threatened, "You'll be left behind;"
When bored with threats profanely rough
We swallow down the poisonous stuff.

Some stand the journey well, and some
Are by the hardships overcome;
And thus the "Mormons" are worn out
Upon this long and weary route.

On November 1 Adjutant Dykes resigned
his position and my old friend Philemon C.
Merrill, who was acting as Second Lieutenant
of Company B, was appointed adjutant of the

Battalion, which change gave general satisfaction to all of us.

We found the judgment of Colonel Cooke good in traveling. He never crowded the men unnecessarily, but as the roads got so much worse that both men and teams failed fast, our only hope of reaching California lay in our faith in God, and on pulling at the ropes.

On November 3 Brother James Hampton, who had been on sick list, was reported by Dr. Sanderson as ready for duty, but so far from being well, he died about 2 o'clock in the afternoon of the same day. He was a faithful soldier and worthy Latter-day Saint. When it was learned that he was dying a halt of about twenty minutes was made, and after his death he was placed in a wagon and taken to our next camping place, where he was buried.

The same day we received

Orders No. 14.

The commanding officer feels it his duty, on the report of his principal guide, for the safety of the Battalion, to make further reduction of its rations. Hereafter ten ounces of pork will be issued as the ration, and nine ounces of flour. Fresh meat will be issued at a pound and a half.

By order of
LIEUT. COL. COOKE, Com.
P. C. MERRILL, Adjt.

THE MORMON BATTALION.

By Eliza R. Snow.

When "Mormon" trains were journeying through
To Winter Quarters, from Nauvoo,
Five hundred men were called to go
To settle claims with Mexico—
To fight for that same Government
From which, as fugitives, we went.
What were their families to do—
Their children, wives, and mothers, too,
When fathers, husbands, sons were gone?
Mothers drove teams, and camps moved on.

And on the brave Battalion went
With Colonel Allen who was sent
As officer of Government.
The noble Colonel Allen knew
His "Mormon boys" were brave and true,
And he was proud of his command
As he led forth his "Mormon Band."

He sickened, died, and they were left
Of a loved leader soon bereft!

And his successor proved to be
The embodiment of cruelty.
Lieutenant Smith, the tyrant, led
The cohort on, in Allen's stead,
To Santa Fe, where Colonel Cooke
The charge of the Battalion took.

'Twas well the vision of the way
Was closed before them on the day
They started out for Santa Fe!
'Tis said no infantry till then,
E'er suffered equal to those men.
Their beeves were famished and their store
Was nigh exhausted long before
They reached the great Pacific shore.
Teams e'en fell dead upon the road,
While soldiers helped to draw the load!

'Twas cruel, stern necessity
That prompted such severity;
For General Kearney in command
Of army in the western land
Expressly ordered Colonel Cooke,
The man who failure could not brook,
To open up a wagon road
Where wheels, till then, had never trod;
And Colonel Cooke was in command
Across the desert waste and sand:
He, with a staunch and iron will,
The general's orders to fulfill,

Must every nerve and sinew strain
The expedition's point to gain.
Tho' stern, and e'en at times morose,
Strict sense of justice marked his course.
He, as his predecessors, knew
The "Mormon" men were firm and true.

They found roadmaking worse by far
Than all the horrors of the war;
Tried by the way—when they got through
They'd very little more to do;
The opposing party, panic struck,
Dare not compete with "Mormon" pluck,
And off in all directions fled—
No charge was fired—no blood was shed.

Our God who rules in worlds of light
Controls by wisdom and by might,
If need, His purpose to fulfill,
He moves the nations at His will—
The destinies of men o'er-rules,
And uses whom He will as tools.
The wise can see and understand,
While fools ignore His guiding hand.

Ere the Battalion started out
Upon that most important route,
'Twas thus predicted by the tongue
Of the Apostle Brigham Young:
"If to your God and country true,
You'll have no fighting there to do."

Was General Kearney satisfied?
Yes, more—for he with martial pride
Said, "O'er the Alps Napoleon went,
But these men cross'd a continent."

And thus, with God Almighty's aid,
The conquest and the road were made,
By which a threatened storm was stayed
And lo! the Saints of God were saved.

While traveling on the 4th, two soldiers
were tied behind an ox wagon and obliged to
march in that position through wind and dust,
for neglecting to get up and salute Lieutenant
Dykes, while he was visiting the guards the
previous night.

On November 6 we arrived at the place
where General Kearney had left his wagons,
and from this point he had gone on with pack-
animals. We were to open a wagon road from
here to the coast. Besides what we had pre-
viously endured from hunger and having to
help our worn-out animals pull the overloaded
wagons, we now would have the additional task
of constructing a wagon road over a wild, desert country.

The next day some one killed a black-tailed deer, which was a rich treat to our hungry company.

On the 10th a detachment of fifty-five sick men under the command of Lieutenant W. W. Willis was sent back to Pueblo to winter. Twelve of these were from Company C. We parted from these brethren with many prayers and much anxiety for their safety, then turned again to the work before us which was not a very pleasing picture, but our trust was in our Heavenly Father.

Colonel Cooke issued an order to leave here the two remaining ox wagons; the commanders of companies were also required to reduce their number of tents to one for nine instead of six men, and all upright poles and the extra camp kettles to be left. We did some packing of both oxen and mules. It was laughable to see the antics of our frightened animals. They bellowed and snorted, pawed and plowed the ground with their horns, whirling and jumping—as some of the boys said, "they kicked up before and reared up behind." Even our sedate commander said "they were irresistibly ludicrous, jumping high from the ground in double quickstep time, turning around the while—a perfect jig."

On the 11th we marched fifteen miles. I was one of those who had charge of the mules. Colonel Cooke, seeing a patch of willows and cane grass, rode into it, and following down the bottom for nearly a mile, found water and grass plentiful. We camped on the bluff, and tried our commander's new invention of using our muskets for tent poles.

The 15th of November was stormy, snow and rain falling at intervals, and being Sunday, we concluded to lay by on the banks of a small stream. We slaughtered an old ox which had given out; though he was a mere skeleton, his remaining flesh was issued as rations.

Passing around the base of the mountain, the next day, to a narrow canyon, we found a marshy water hole which we named Cooke's Spring, a name which it still bears. Here we found California quail; we also killed a couple of goats, and we regarded all these luxuries as gifts from our Heavenly Father.

We next traveled over the "table land" and

this part of the country can hardly be excelled for beauty of landscape. Elevated to the highest of these tables or flats, no matter which way you cast the eye, a most beautiful, grassy plain stretches out as far as you can see.

On the 20th we lay by, our guides having gone twelve miles ahead, and not being able to see any water or any indications of water, had returned disheartened, thinking no water would be found short of the Gila River—over a hundred miles. Our commander called a council and the decision was to follow a road leading in a southwesterly direction, through settlements where we hoped to obtain food and fresh teams.

When this decision was made known a gloom was cast over us, for we wanted to go on to California. But at this juncture Father Pettigrew and Brother Hancock went from tent to tent and in a low voice counseled us to "pray to the Lord to change the Colonel's mind." That night over three hundred fervent prayers ascended to the throne of grace for that one favor.

The next morning the command continued

the journey for about two miles, when it was found that the road began to bear directly for Old Mexico. Colonel Cooke halted, looked all around, rose in his saddle and ordered a halt. He then said with firmness: "This is not my course. I was ordered to California; and," he added with an oath, "I will go there or die in the attempt!" Then to the bugler, "Blow the right." Father Pettigrew involuntarily exclaimed, "God bless the Colonel!" and as the Colonel's keen penetrating eyes glanced in the direction of the voice, his stern face for once softened and he looked pleased.

We felt that our prayers were answered and the next day we traveled about eighteen miles and camped without water. Here it was decided and ordered that the men walk in double file in front of the wagons and tramp a trail for the wheels—each company leading for an hour and then falling to the rear; this made all have an equal share in the hard work. This plan was followed in traveling over all the heavy, sandy road, until we reached the coast; it was very hard on us as we had no road or trail to follow.

On the 23rd we came to a hole or crevice in a rock where there was a little water but the Colonel and staff rode up to it and their mules drained it. When we came up some looked at it wistfully and passed on, while some dipped with spoons what they could get. Then a guide came back telling us of water about nine miles ahead of us. After dark we found water in some swamp holes.

Next day we rested as most of us were exhausted. From here a company of pioneers was sent forward to work a road over the backbone of the Rocky Mountains.

On the 28th we reached the summit of the Rocky Mountains, where we found plenty of deer, bear, antelope and small game.

The next day we prepared for descending the mountains. We packed the animals and sent them down into the valley, about six miles, where a guard was left with the baggage while the men and animals returned, and the work of taking the wagons down was commenced. Long ropes were tied to the wagons, and the men held back on them; thus the wagons were lowered. During the three days that we encamped on the mountain the weather was very cold but when we got into the valley, it was mild and pleasant, and the scenery was beautiful.

On the 2nd of December we reached the ruins of the old Rancho San Bernardino where we rested a day and a half and hunted wild cattle, thus adding five days rations to our scanty supplies.

Before breaking camp orders were issued to the effect that "Commanders of companies hereafter will give no permission to leave the column of march or the camp, and muskets will not be fired at game;" and also a verbal order that we were to have no loaded guns in the command, which last order was not strictly obeyed.

Thus we marched, from twelve to seventeen miles a day, sometimes in a snow storm or rain, often camping without wood or water, and on the 9th we nooned at San Pedro creek, where the grass looked as though it was dry straw but it proved to be splendid feed.

Continuing our journey down the San Pedro we encamped on the night of the 11th in a canyon, where occurred the famous "Bull Fight" which is so well described by our musician, Brother Hancock:

THE BULL FIGHT ON THE SAN PEDRO.

Under command of Colonel Cooke,
When passing down San Pedro's brook,
Where cane-grass, growing rank and high,
Was waving as the breeze pass'd by:

There, as we gained ascending ground,
Out from the grass, with fearful bound,
A wild, ferocious bull appear'd,
And challenged fight, with horns uprear'd.

"Stop, stop!" said one, "just see that brute!"
"Hold!" was responded, "let me shoot."
He flashed, but failed to fire the gun—
Both stood their ground, and would not run.

The man exclaimed, "I want some meat;
I think that bull will do to eat."
And saying thus, again he shot
And fell'd the creature on the spot.

It soon arose to run away,
And then the guns began to play:
All hands at work—amid the roar,
The bull was dropp'd to rise no more.

But lo!. it did not end the fight—
A furious herd rushed into sight,
And then the bulls and men around
Seemed all resolved to stand their ground.
 *   *   *   *   *   *
The bulls with madden'd fury raged—
The men a skillful warfare waged:
Tho' some, from danger had to flee,
And hide or clamber up a tree.

A bull at one man made a pass,
Who hid himself amid the grass,
And breathless lay until the brute
Passed him and took another shoot.

The bulls rushed on like unicorns
And gored the mules with piercing horns,
As if the battle ground to gain,
When men and mules should all be slain. ·
 *   *   *   *   *   *
A. Cox from one bull's horns was thrown
Ten feet in air: when he came down,
A gaping flesh wound met his eye—
The vicious beast had gored his thigh.*

---

*"Brother Amos Cox had a terrible cut in his
thigh, about eight inches long, near the groin, by
a bull's horn. The doctor sewed it up but he was
an invalid for a long time."—P. C. Merrill Autobiography.

The Colonel and his staff were there,
Mounted, and witnessing the war;
A bull, one hundred yards away,
Eyed Colonel Cooke as easy prey.

But Corp'ral Frost stood bravely by,
And watch'd the bull with steady eye;
The brute approach'd near and more near,
But Frost betray'd no sign of fear.

The Colonel ordered him to run;
Unmoved he stood with loaded gun;
The bull came up with daring tread,
When near his feet, Frost shot him dead *

Whatever cause, we did not know,
But something prompted them to go;
When all at once in frantic fright,
The bulls ran bellowing out of sight.

---

*"The corporal was on foot while the Colonel
and his staff were mounted. On the first approach of the bull, the Colonel with his usual firm
manner, ordered the corporal to load his gun. To
this command he ~aid no attention. Thinking him
stupid, he ordered him to run, but he did not
move. Frost aimed his musket very deliberately,
and only fired when the bull was within six paces,
and it fell headlong almost at his feet. He had
stood firm at the risk of his own life to protect
his brave but austere commander, thus showing a
brave, generous and forgiving heart, and Colonel
Cooke said 'he was one of the bravest men I
ever saw.' "—Mormon Battalion History.

And when the fearful fight was o'er,
And sound of muskets heard no more,
At least a score of bulls were found
And two mules dead upon the ground.

We followed on down the river and soon
passed near the base of the mountains which
extend towards the Gila River, traveling nearly
north. Our orders now were:

* * * * * We will march to Tucson.
We came not to make war on Sonora, and less
still to destroy an important outpost of de-
fense against the Indians; but we will take the
straight road before us and overcome all re-
sistance. But shall I remind you that the
American soldier ever shows justice and kindness to the unarmed and unresisting? The
property of individuals you will hold sacred.
The people of Sonora are not our enemies.
      By order of
                  LIEUT. COL. COOKE,
      (Signed)   P. C. MERRILL, Adjutant.

After traveling some eight or nine miles
we struck a trail leading to Tuscon. Our Colonel learned here from some Mexican soldiers
that great excitement prevailed at Tucson be-

cause it was rumored there that a large force of American soldiers was approaching the fort. A message was therefore sent to Colonel Comaduran at the post, that the people need not be alarmed, as we were their friends and would do them no harm, but would simply purchase some supplies and pass on.

When near the post about a dozen well-armed men, in citizens' dress, met and accompanied us to the town. Before passing through the gate a halt was called, and Colonel Cooke stated that the citizens and soldiers had deserted the town leaving their property behind them, and although it was in our power there must be no interference with private property.

CHAPTER VI.

ON TO THE PACIFIC.

A Midnight Alarm—Unfortunate Attempt to Nav-
igate the Gila—First Sight of the Ocean—Safe
at San Diego—Col. Cooke's Classic Congratula-
tions.

WHEN we marched through the deserted
streets of Tucson some aged men and
some women and children brought us water,
thus showing us respect and kindness. We
made no halt in the town but traveled down
the stream about a half mile and camped.
Colonel, Cooke returned to the post and obtained some public wheat for feeding our
teams, and also some salt which we had been
without for several days.

About midnight we were roused by signal
guns being fired; then we heard Lieutenant
George Oman calling excitedly: "Beat that
drum, beat that drum—if you can't beat that
drum, beat that fife!" then ordered every man

7

into line; campfires were replenished and the music began playing a lively tune, while each company formed into column; when suddenly the stern voice of Colonel Cooke ordered "Cease that music! Dust those lights!" This was instantly done and he stationed us on either side of the road about ten feet apart.

Here we stood while a party was sent on ahead to see what was the trouble. They were gone so long that another detachment with Brother Reddick Allred at their head was sent to look after their safety. In about an hour all parties returning and nothing seeming to be alarming we were allowed to retire, being instructed to have our arms in easy reach and to remember our places. Nothing further came to alarm, and we felt that the prophecy of Brigham Young was being fulfilled as "we had seen no fighting except with wild beasts."

On the next day we moved onward, and at 9 o'clock we camped without water, having traveled twenty-four miles. Some of our worn-out famished men came straggling into camp at all hours of the night, and in the morning all who were able traveled on, over a kind of

baked clay with occasional sand beds to pull
through. Company C was in the rear of the
others and Lieutenant Rosecrans left his men
and rode into the hills in search of water, and
found a hole some distance from the road. He
took the foremost of us to it, then filled their
canteens, rode back to the famishing men, gave
us what water he had and led us to the spring.
We drank our fill but the water soon became
muddy, but we cooked a few provisions and
went on to overtake the command, which we
did about 3 o'clock in the morning, having
passed many brethren lying by the way beg-
ging for water.

The advance struck water and camped about
noon the next day, and several took mules and
canteens and came back to relieve the sufferings of their comrades, and thus doubtless
saved the lives of many of us. All the afternoon the poor straggling men came into camp.

When we reached the Gila River we made a
halt, and while here hundreds of Pima Indians
came into our camps. They seemed to be honest and industrious and glad to see us. We
went through one village of them containing

near four thousand inhabitants, peaceable and contented, engaged in agriculture and making blankets.

Here we traded buttons (cut from our clothes) for cakes of bread—and also some old clothing for corn, beans, molasses, squash, etc. —but in the evening our Colonel ordered all private provisions which could not be carried by the owners to be left on the ground. This seemed pretty hard when we were on only half rations, but a great deal was left.

On the 23rd and 24th of December we camped at a village of Maricopa Indians, having traveled over a beautiful plain of rich, cultivated land. Here it was that Colonel Cooke suggested to our senior officer that this vicinity would be a good place for the exiled Saints to locate; which suggestion was very favorably received by the Indians.

We spent Christmas day by marching eighteen miles from Maricopa village, mainly up hill and over sand, and then camped without water. The following day we advanced twenty-three miles and camped near the Gila. We had followed around the base of a mountain

and crossed a bend in the river. Our route
would have been much shorter could we have
gone in a more direct line.

We now traveled very slowly as the way was
over heavy sandy bottoms, and sometimes
quicksand; we only made sixty miles in six
days, and even then the men had to work hard
at helping the mules pull the loads.

As we traveled down the river we found rock
covered with ancient hieroglyphics, including
profiles of men, beasts and reptiles. Grass was
very scarce and the 1st of January, 1847, we
cut down cottonwood trees for our animals to
browse upon. A number of our mules died
showing strong symptoms of poison, but we
did not know where they got it.

Colonel Cooke here hit upon a novel plan to
convey part of our luggage and relieve the
tired teams. He prepared a boat of two pontoon wagon-bodies lashed together, end to end,
between two dry cottonwood logs, and this cu-
rious barge was loaded with twenty-five hundred pounds of provisions for the men and corn
for the mules. This cast a gloom over us for we
felt that there ought not to be any risks taken

with our already scanty supplies. But our boat was put out into the river and after having some trouble getting it over a sand-bar we saw nothing of it for several days.

Now we were ordered to have another reduction of rations—one ounce to the man. Several of the men had already fainted from hunger and exhaustion, and it seemed that a few more reductions would leave nothing.

On the 8th of January we reached the mouth of the Gila River. In the absence of grass our mules were fed mesquite-beans; and we ground the beans in our coffee-mills and made cakes of the meal; it tasted quite delicious to us starving men.

On the 9th a march of ten miles, sometimes in heavy sand and sometimes in miry clay, brought us to the crossing of the Colorado, which was muddy like the Missouri, quite as wide but not as deep as that river. Here we were overtaken by those who had been sent back to recover the provisions left on the Gila from the barge: they had found only four hundred pounds of flour but no pork.

All the next day and night we spent ferrying

the river in pontoon wagon-boxes. Two mules
were drowned while being driven across. Company C's wagon got stuck on the sand-bar in
the river, between the two channels, with a
broken-down team. The Colonel refused to
allow the other companies to wait or render
us any assistance, but proceeded on with them.
So, in order to extricate the wagon from the
quicksand, we had to do as we had done in the
desert, get out and help pull, though we were
half-starved, and worn out through the
Colonel's indiscretion in losing our food by the
boat disaster. Our team was so broken down
that a few miles further on the wagon had
to be abandoned.

On the 15th we marched seven miles and
reached a well called "Pozo Hondo," which
afforded us but a little very poor water; it
served however to save life until better could
be reached. Here, one of our guides, who had
been sent ahead of us to purchase fresh mules
and beef cattle, met us with thirty-five mules
in good condition and ten fat beeves. We
were not long in killing one of the latter animals, and it was a great treat to us.

The Indians call this region "the hot land," which name is very appropriate, for it is by far the hottest country I ever saw: an almost tropical sun in day time and a December atmosphere at night, which was very hurtful and weakening to us and our animals; our clothing was very scanty and some of us suffered severely from the cold nights.

Words cannot describe our situation at this time; it was very trying for both men and mules. Here we found the heaviest sand, the hottest days and the coldest nights, with no water and little food; we were nearly bare-footed, some using rawhide wrapped around their feet, others wrapped cast-off clothing around to protect their feet from the burning sand.

When we arrived at Cariza, a small creek, we called it "first running water." Many of us were so nearly used up from thirst, hunger and fatigue that we could not speak until we had a cup of water. About sixteen mules gave out and our fresh ones were nearly exhausted.

On the 17th we traveled fifteen miles over very heavy sand, and camped between two mountains. "Completely worn down, some staggering as they walked, others, unable to keep up with the wagons, slept and traveled at intervals and did not reach camp until daylight the next morning. I went through the companies and found them eating their last four ounces of flour; of sugar and coffee, there had been none for some weeks."*

During the day we received a letter from the governor of San Diego, promising us assistance. We did not advance on the 18th but spent the day cleaning up our arms, and in the evening the men were paraded and inspected. The Colonel expressed great surprise at seeing us singing merry songs and playing the fiddle when we were so wornout and hungry, but we were thankful to our Heavenly Father and rejoiced that our journey was nearly finished and the night air was full of the songs of the Saints.

On the 19th we had a hard travel up hill, over a mountain ridge, up a dry ravine, through openings in the solid rocks. Our guides knew no more about this route than we did. We followed the ravine until we found ourselves in a passage at least a foot narrower

---

*Colonel Cooke's diary.

than our wagons. Our tools were nearly all
lost by the boat disaster, but we had a few axes,
a crowbar and a spade or two. With these we
set to·work, Colonel Cooke taking an ax and
helping us. We widened the passage and got
our wagons through about sundown, when we
found that water was seven or eight miles further on, so we traveled till dark and camped
without water, but had good grass for the
animals.

On the night of the 20th we camped with
plenty of water—a blessing which we all ap-
preciated.

We now received orders to march directly to
San Diego instead of Los Angeles as we had
intended.

On the 21st we came to Warner's rancho,
this being the first house we had seen since
entering California. The weather was cold and
cloudy and looked like snow. We crossed the
mountain ridge dividing the waters of the
Colorado and the gulf from those emptying into the Pacific. We camped about 2 p. m. and
were met here by those who had gone ahead
for supplies and here we had a full meal which

consisted of fresh, fat beef, without salt, and a few pancakes purchased from the Indians. Here our rations were raised to four pounds of beef a day, but we had no other food, not even salt, until on the 23rd, those who had been sent back for our lost provisions came in with about four hundred pounds of flour. That was a little more than a pound for a man, and we usually used about two spoonfuls each day to thicken our soup.

We had very heavy rain for two days before leaving Warner's. Some mules strayed away, but a friendly Indian—Chief Antonio—gathered them up for us.

On January 25 we received a dispatch from General Kearney, ordering us to meet him in San Diego, so we were again on the march, reaching the Temecula Valley that day. Here the San Luis Rey Indians mistook us for a band of Californians and both parties were drawn up in battle array before the mistake was discovered. Then the Indians were pleased to see us and the chief men shook hands heartily with Colonel Cooke and others.

We passed through the San Luis Rey Valley and found grass from two to ten inches high and plenty of wild mustard whose young, tender leaves made splendid greens, which we enjoyed with our beef. We also saw thousands of wild geese, ducks and gulls.

We arrived at San Luis Rey, a deserted Catholic mission, about noon on January 27, and on climbing a bluff near the mission the long, long-looked-for Pacific Ocean was before us. The joy that filled our souls none but wornout pilgrims nearing a haven of rest can imagine. As we stood on its borders, looking at its beauty, admiring its peaceful serenity, a cheer arose from our hearts and found utterance as one voice, and we forgot that we were hungry, ragged, barefooted or far from home, and we gave thanks to God who had preserved our lives amid such sufferings and had enabled us to endure to the end of this perilous journey; and we prayed for the safety and comfort of our loved ones whom we had left so far away. But we knew that He would care for His Saints, and we went on our way rejoicing and took up our quarters five miles from San Diego.

We no longer suffered from the hardships of deserts or the cold atmosphere of the snow-capped mountains, for January here was as pleasant as May in the Northern States. We traveled in sight of the ocean, in the mild climate and clear sunshine, with wild oats, grass and mustard growing luxuriously around us; the soil being very rich and the water clear and good; the birds sang sweetly and our hearts were happy as we joined all nature in praising the Giver of all good; and on the 29th we came in sight of the long-talked-of San Diego. We camped at the old Catholic mission and for the first time in our lives saw olives, date and other palm trees.

We had traveled about one thousand four hundred miles in one hundred and four days, and after enduring so much suffering, it cheered our hearts to hear the following orders, which were read to us on February 4— and were received with a hearty cheer by the Battalion: ·

HEADQUARTERS MORMON BATTALION,
MISSION OF SAN DIEGO,
JAN. 30, 1847.

Orders No. 1.

The Lieut. Col. commanding congratulates the Battalion on their safe arrival on the shore of the Pacific Ocean and the conclusion of their march, of over two thousand miles.

History may be searched in vain for an equal march of infantry. Half of it has been through a wilderness where nothing but savages and wild beasts are found, or deserts, where, for want of water, there is no living creature. There, with almost hopeless labor we have dug deep wells, which the future traveler will enjoy. Without a guide who had traversed them, we have ventured into trackless table-lands where water was not found for several marches. With crowbar and pick and ax in hand, we have worked our way over mountains, which seemed to defy aught save the wild goat, and hewed a passage through a chasm of living rock more narrow than our wagons. To bring these first wagons to the Pacific, we have preserved the strength of our mules by herding them over large tracts which you have laboriously guarded without loss. The garrison of four presidios of Sonora concentrated within the walls of Tucson, gave us no pause. We drove them out, with their artillery, but our intercourse with the citizens was unmarked by a single act of injustice. Thus, marching half naked and half fed, and living upon wild animals, we have discovered and made a road of great value to our country.

Arrived at the first settlement in California, after a single day's rest, you cheerfully turned off from the route to this point of promised repose, to enter upon a campaign, and meet, as we supposed, the approach of an enemy; and this too without salt to season your sole subsistence of fresh meat.

Lieutenant A. J. Smith and George Stoneman, of the First Dragoons, have shared and given valuable aid in all these labors.

Thus, volunteers, you have exhibited some high and essential qualities of veterans. But much remains undone. Soon you will turn your attention to the drill, to system and order, to forms also, which are all necessary to the soldier.

By order of
LIEUT. COL. P. ST. GEORGE COOKE,
P. C. MERRILL, Adjutant.

CHAPTER VII.

BATTALION MUSTERED OUT.

Religious Services and Daily Routine—Mail Carrier and on Indian Duty—Kearney's Tribute to "Mormons"—Civilian Employment as Ranch Foreman.

WHILE in garrison we made it a rule, when possible, to hold religious services on Sunday, which were presided over by Captain Hunt, Father Pettigrew or Brother Hancock.

Our daily garrison duties were: Roll call at daylight, sick call at 7:30 a. m., breakfast call at 8:40, drill at 10 a. m. and 3 p. m., roll call at sundown, tattoo at 8:30, and taps of the drum at 9 p. m., after which lights must be out except in case of sickness. All must then retire.

While quartered at San Diego, Azariah Smith composed the following song:

HARD TIMES.

In forty-six we bade adieu
To loving friends and kindred too;
For one year's service, one and all
Enlisted at our country's call,
    In these hard times.

We onward marched until we gained
Fort Leavenworth, where we obtained
Our outfit—each a musket drew—
Canteen, knapsack, and money, too—
    In these hard times.

Our colonel died—Smith took his place,
And marched us on at rapid pace;
O'er hills and plains we had to go,
Through herds of deer and buffalo,
    In these hard times.

O'er mountains and through valleys, too,
We town and village went through;
Through forests dense, with mazes twined,
Our tedious steps we had to wind,
    In these hard times.

At length we came to Santa Fe,
As much fatigued as men could be;
With only ten days there to stay,
When orders came to march away,
    In these hard times.

8

Three days and twenty we marched down
Rio Del Norte, past many a town;
Then changed our course—resolved to go
Across the mountains, high or low,
  In these hard times.

We found the mountains very high,
Our patience and our strength to try;
For, on half rations, day by day,
O'er mountain heights we made our way,
  In these hard times.

Some pushed the wagons up the hills,
Some drove the teams, some packed the
   mules,
Some stood on guard by night and day
Lest haplessly our teams should stray,
  In these hard times.

We traveled twenty days or more,
Adown the Gila river's shore—
Crossed o'er the Colorado then,
And marched upon a sandy plain,
  In these hard times.

We thirsted much from day to day,
And mules were dying by the way,
When lo! to view, a glad scene burst,
Where all could quench our burning thirst,
  In these hard times.

We traveled on without delay,
And quartered at San Luis Rey;
We halted there some thirty days,
And now are quartered in this place,
    In these hard times.

A "Mormon" soldier band we are:
May our great Father's watchful care
In safety kindly guide our feet,
Till we again our friends shall meet,
    And have good times.

Oh, yes, we trust to meet our friends
Where truth its light to all extends—
Whose love prevails in every breast,
Throughout the province of the blest,
    And have good times.

While the Battalion was stationed at San Diego, I carried the United States mail from San Luis Rey to Los Angeles and back; but as the presence of soldiers was needed in Los Angeles to hold that place, Companies C, A, D and E took up the line of march for that place, on March 19th, traveling over broken country near the seashore, and arrived there about noon on the 23rd. There were no provisions to be got here and on the 25th, (our supplies which

we had brought with us being nearly exhausted), an eight-mule team was despatched for a
fresh supply from San Diego. I drove the
mules.

On April 6 a petition was circulated and
signed by most of the soldiers, asking for our
discharge, asserting that as peace was declared
our services could now be dispensed with and
we were needed at home to aid our outcast
families; but it was never presented to Colonel
Cooke as some of the officers wished us to enlist again with Captain Hunt as Lieutenant
Colonel.

Owing to the fact that the Californians were
not allowed to bear arms the following orders
were issued for their protection from maraud-
ing bands of Indians:

HEADQUARTERS SOUTHERN MILITARY DISTRICT,
            LOS ANGELES, APRIL 11, 1847.
Orders No. 7.

(1)Company C Mormon Battalion will
march tomorrow and take post in the canyon
pass of the mountains about forty-five miles
eastward of this town. Lieutenant Rosecrans,
its commander, will select a spot for his camp
as near to the narrowest and most defensible

part as the convenience of water, feed and grass will admit of, and, if necessary, effectually to prevent a passage of hostile Indians with or without horses he will erect a sufficient cover of logs or earth. It will be his duty to guard the pass effectually, and, if necessary, to send out armed parties, either on foot or mounted, to defend the ranchos of the vicinity, or to attack wandering parties of wild Indians.

P. St. George Cooke,
Lieut. Col. Commanding.

So on the 12th of April, Company C marched to Cajon Pass, where we remained until we were relieved by Lieutenant Pace's detachment on the 23rd, when we returned to Los Angeles.

Although despised by many, the dragoons were always our staunch friends, and often when bullies came into town and began to impose upon the "Mormon boys," the dragoons would not allow us to take our own part, but would say: "Stand back! you are religious men and we are not; we will take all of your fights into our hands, and you shall not be imposed upon by them."

On the 9th of May General Kearney (ac-

companied by Colonel Stevenson and other officers of note) arrived at Los Angeles from
Monterey; and on the 10th he addressed the
Battalion. He dwelt at some length upon our
arduous journey, our patriotism to the government, obedience to orders, etc. No commander
could ever have given more praise to any corps
of veterans than was given us by this grand old
Colonel. He sympathized with us in the unset-
tled condition of our people, said he would take
pleasure in representing our patriotism to the
President and in the halls of Congress, and
give us the justice our praiseworthy conduct
had merited. He said history might be searched
in vain for a march equal to ours—while
"Bonaparte crossed the Alps, these men have
crossed a continent."

A number of our men now re-enlisted for
six months—being promised at the end of that
time, pay and rations to San Francisco or to
Bear River Valley, with a detachment to act
as pioneers for them; we were also promised
that we might obtain work and earn money
whenever off duty. Accordingly I obtained a
furlough and engaged work with a Mr. Wil-

liams who owned a large ranch of several hundreds of acres and great herds of cattle and horses; also a large soap factory.

On July 15, 1847, we went into Los Angeles and the next day at 3 o'clock p. m. the five companies of the Battalion were formed in line according to letter of company, A in front and E in rear.   Lieutenant A. J. Smith then marched down and back between the lines and said in a low voice: "You are discharged." None of the men regretted his brevity: in fact it rather pleased us.

On the 20th, having drawn my pay, I returned to Chino ranch, where I worked as foreman for Williams for about a year and a half; the work was easy, for my horse was saddled for me in the morning and all I had to do was to ride around and see that the men kept at their work and followed orders.

And now I will leave the Battalion by quoting a song about them which was composed by Thomas Morris and is much liked by all our people.

MORMON BATTALION.

All hail the brave Battalion!
   The noble, valiant band,
That went and served our country
   With willing heart and hand.
Altho' we're called disloyal
   By many a tongue and pen,
Our nation boasts no soldiers
   So true as "Mormon" men.

O'er many a barren desert
   Our weary feet have trod,
To find where, unmolested,
   The Saints can worship God.
We've built up many cities—
   We're building temples, too;
Which prove to all beholders
   What "Mormon" hands can do.

We settled here in Utah
   Upon a sterile soil,
And by our faith and patience
   And hard, unflinching toil,
And thro' the daily blessings
   Our Father, God, bestows,
The once forbidding desert
   Now blossoms as the rose.

What tho' the wicked hate us,
    And 'gainst our rights contend;
And, through their vile aggressions,
    Our brotherhood would rend?
The keys of truth and knowledge
    And power to us belong;
And we'll extend our borders
    And make our bulwarks strong.

Our sons are growing mighty,
    And they are spreading forth,
To multiply our numbers
    And beautify the earth.
All hail, the brave Battalion!
    The noble, valiant band,
That went and served our country
    With willing heart and hand.

CHAPTER VIII.

LIFE IN CALIFORNIA.

Visit to England—Across the Plains to Salt Lake
—Successes in Business—Marriages and Births
—Seven Eventful Years.

IN the spring of 1849 I went to Sutter's
ranch and worked in the gold diggings, but
as that kind of work did not suit me at all I
only stayed three days. I then broke mules—
that is, I taught them to pack, for a while, then
went back to Southern California and there
bought a band of horses at $1.50 a head and
started for San Francisco, selling some along
the way, and realized a hundred dollars apiece
for them.

One day, while riding, my horse fell on me
and broke my leg. A family by the name of
Otterson—a widow and two daughters—took
care of me for three months; they were good

people and they were very kind to me. When
I was able to walk on crutches I sold the remaining horses; gave one to each of the Otterson girls (with a saddle and bridle), and to
their mother I gave two horses, a buggy and
harness. Then I bought a ticket for England, but before I went on shipboard, I sent
my money (which was a large amount) to the
Bank of England and also a letter to my folks,
telling them how to obtain it if I never arrived.

I went on board the vessel "James Pennell"
—still on crutches, and sailed by way of Cape
Horn and arrived in Liverpool in March, 1850,
without any accidents or incidents and found
my money all right.

After paying my tithing to Apostle Orson
Pratt, I went to my old home, and found that
my mother had been dead two weeks.

On May 3, 1850, in Sandy church, Bedfordshire, Sarah Martin and I were married by the
Rev. Cook.

There were many of the Saints in England
who were anxious to come to Utah, but had
not means to do so; I therefore engaged passage for them on the ship "James Pennell,"

and on October 2, 1850, we set sail from our native land for America, as I had done seven years before. In our company was my wife, my father—Samuel Layton—a young lady—Sarah Barnes—a companion of my wife, and a niece of ours—Priscilla Martin. There were also two hundred and fifty more Saints on the ship of whom I had the charge.

After seven weeks tossing on the ocean we arrived at New Orleans, November 22, and took the steamer "Amaranth" up the river to St. Louis, arriving there December 4.

Apostle Orson Hyde counseled me to stay here and rent a farm that I might employ the men who had come over with me, and thus give them an opportunity to pay the money back. Therefore I settled my family in St. Louis, on Fourth and Poplar streets, for the winter. I rented Mr. McPherson's farm south of Bellefontaine Cemetery in the spring, built a house and moved my family out there.

On May 1, 1857, a son was born to us, and we named him William, but in August that year the little one had chills and fever, and died.

In the spring of 1852 I started with my
family for Salt Lake City, Utah, but while
camped in the woods near Kansas City, Mo.,
I received word to go to Lexington, Mo. to
aid in purchasing cattle for the first (English)
emigration company. I therefore went, purchased the cattle, left them at Kearney's ranch,
returned to my family and took them to the
ranch—having been absent from the family
about three weeks. The company having encamped at Keokuk preparatory to crossing
the plains, was under the charge of A. O.
Smoot, as captain, and I was appointed his
assistant; but after the company started Brother Smoot was taken very sick with cholera and
I was given entire charge of the company.

As we were journeying on over the plains
we met Apostles John Taylor, Ezra T. Benson and Jedediah Grant, who were on their
way East, so we camped and they remained
with us for three days, and each night we held
a meeting. The singing was furnished by
three young ladies from England. We had a
good time and our spiritual strength was renewed while we went on our way rejoicing.

The Spirit of the Lord was with us in our journey and no lives were lost nor any one hurt, although we passed through many dangerous experiences, and arrived in Salt Lake City September 3, 1852, with fifty-two wagons.

While at Red Butte we were met by President Brigham Young, and he said: "If that ain't the best outfit that ever landed in Salt Lake!"

I had brought with me a new threshing machine (one of the first, if not the very first, in Utah); three new wagons; one carriage; several head of good horses; one hundred head of stock—some of which were blooded Durhams. I set up the machine at once and put the men at work threshing grain; turned the stock out on west Jordan range for the winter and bought a house in the Fifteenth ward on First South and Fourth West streets, and built a large room on it in which to store the grain.

On September 26, 1852, Sarah Barnes and I were married, at Salt Lake City.

In October I went to West Jordan, built a

shanty about a mile from the river, and moved the family over on November 9, 1852. The snow was so deep, it drove before the axle of the wagon and when we reached our home, the snow which had been melting was dripping from the house and there was not a dry place to be found on the floor. I went down to the river and cut willows and carried them to the house on my back. Then I climbed on the roof, one of my wives handing the willows up to me and I spread them out on the roof; after which we threw dirt on them to keep out the water. I brought willows from the river and while they were green, my father would tie them into bundles for fuel. The winter was very severe and our winter's wood consisted of these willow bundles and a few slabs which I bought at Gardner's mill, for twenty-five cents each.

One night we had a severe snow storm from the north; we heard a pitiful "whinney" and when I got up to see what was the matter, I found a favorite blooded mare standing at the door as if asking mercy from the driving storm. I let her inside and there she stayed until the storm was over. No doubt this saved her life.

The year 1852 was notable, not only for continued extension and the growth of Utah settlements, but also for improvements of different kinds projected and forwarded at various points. Mountains of coal and iron were discovered in southern Utah; a fine quality of beautiful white building stone was found near Manti, Sanpete County. This year our people sent a block of the Manti rock to the Washington Monument. It was three feet long, two feet wide and six and a half inches thick. In the center was carved a bee-hive and under it the word "Deseret," and over the hive was the All-Seeing Eye—the whole surmounted and flanked by foliage, beautifully wrought by the chisel of William Ward.

Many new buildings were erected—a woolen mill and sugar factory, cutlery works and potteries were also started.

On New Year's day 1853, the Social Hall in Salt Lake City was dedicated.

On January 1, 1853, Sarah M. gave birth to another son, to whom we gave the name

of Christopher. Beginning about four o'clock
that afternoon, the rain continued to fall all
night. As our roof leaked we covered the
mother and new baby with an oil-skin over-
coat and raised a large umbrella over them.
We also kept up a fire all night and as everything was very wet, whenever the room would
get warm the steam would rise until we could
scarcely see across the room. The blessing of
the Lord rested upon us, however, and in two
or three weeks all were again well and had
felt no inconvenience from our steam bath:
surely "God tempers the blast to the shorn
lamb."

Here is inserted a copy of a

PATRIARCHIAL BLESSING,

Given in Great Salt Lake City, March 16,
1853, by John Smith, Patriarch, upon the head
of Christopher Layton, son of Samuel and
Isabel Layton, born at Bedfordshire, England, March 8, 1820:

I lay my hands upon your head in the name
of Jesus Christ and seal upon you a father's
blessing, even all the blessings that were be-

8

stowed upon Abraham, Isaac, and Jacob, and
the children of Israel in Egypt for you are of
the blood of Joseph and a lawful heir to the
everlasting priesthood, which shall be sealed
upon you in fullness in the due time of the
Lord, teaching you the principles of the priesthood and mysteries that have been kept hid
from before the foundations of the world. You
are appointed to preach the gospel to nations
afar off, to the islands of the sea, to kings,
rulers, and great men of the earth; they shall
obey thy voice; you shall baptize many and
bring them to Zion with vast stores of riches;
baptize many that sail in ships, have power
over the waters to turn them whichsoever way
thou wilt. You shall be blessed in your family with health, peace and plenty—they shall
increase like Jacob. Be mighty in the priesthood; you shall be a counselor in Zion and
preside over one of her stakes; have wisdom
to conduct all affairs in the best possible way;
are to see the winding up scenes of this generation; see wickedness swept from the earth,
Zion re-established in peace, no more to be
thrown down! Finally you shall inherit all the
blessings of the Redeemer's Kingdom for ever.
Amen.

In the spring of 1853 I sold my place to
Wm. Price (now bishop of Goshen) and built

another small house near Gardner's mill and moved the family thither. I also built a milk house as we milked a number of cows, and during the summer my wives made and sold $20 worth of butter, and with that bought furniture for the house. In August I moved the family into Salt Lake, and having business at Fort Bridger I went to that place, and was gone a few weeks.

On September 8, 1853, a son was born to my wife, Sarah B., in Salt Lake City, and we gave him the name of Hyrum John. I built a butcher shop near the Globe Bakery on Main street, and here we lived until the spring of 1854.

On the 12th of December I received in Salt Lake City the papers which made me a citizen of the United States—the country of my adoption.

Going to the Jordan range I built another house and moved part of the family out there in 1854, but during the summer I sold all of my stock and bought some lots on Emigration street—half a block west of State road—and built a good adobe house—a two story one—

on one of these lots, and had another butcher shop at the residence.

In December, 1854, Isabella Golightly and I were married in Salt Lake City, President Brigham Young officiating.

In the spring of 1855 I started two butcher shops, and was greatly assisted in this business by my family. During the emigration season we sold as high as eleven beeves a week, and in order that there might be nothing wasted or lost, my wives made soap and candles out of the fat and tallow. Sometimes we made $100 worth of soap in a week, and twelve pounds of tallow candles in a day.

We always made a point of remembering the poor, the widows and missionaries' wives in Salt Lake City.

In the fall, as the people were getting very much in my debt, I closed up my butcher shops, being so advised by President Young, and bought a farm from S. M. Blair, at Grantsville, Tooele County, he having purchased my Salt Lake property. I moved the family out to the farm. During the summer of 1855, my wife Sarah M. gave birth to a stillborn baby girl, caused by a fall into a cellar. Here, on December 6, 1855, my wife Isabella G. gave birth to a son, whom we named John Henry.

On February 18, 1856, my wife, Sarah B., gave birth to a daughter, whom we named Mary Ann.

On April 12, 1856, Caroline Cooper and I were married at Salt Lake City, President Brigham Young officiating.

CHAPTER IX.

PIONEERING IN CARSON VALLEY.

Perils of the Journey—Brigham Young's Promise
—Labors in Carson—Called back to Utah—
Thrilling Experiences—At Home Again.

HAVING been called with many others to
migrate to Carson Valley, I began to get
things arranged for going away. I had not
been on the farm long enough to realize any
benefit from it. I made a trade with a Mr.
Cooley for a hundred head of cattle and some
money: so that by the end of April we were
ready to travel. My families began to think
we were like the pilgrims of old and had no
certain dwelling place.

Our company consisted of the families of
Wm. Jennings, Wm. Nixon, Peregrine Sessions, Albert P. Dewey, Wm. Kay, Geo. Neb-
eker, and my own family.

We camped at Black Rock the second night
out, and in the morning we found several

inches of snow on the ground, which made
it rather unpleasant for the babies, but the
women all took matters cheerfully and we had
our breakfast, and traveled on. We camped
at Warm Springs at Kay's Creek one night;
nothing happened of much moment, except
one or two nights the cattle started back home,
thus delaying us somewhat.

While we were camped on Bear River, we
met President Young and company who were
going to explore Bear Lake Valley.

Brother Brigham remarked: "Brother Layton, you have more stock than the whole
Church." "Brother Young, they are all at
your disposal," I answered. "Oh, no. I don't
want them," he said. So I picked out ten
head of my best cows and made him a present of them. President Young then blessed me
and my family and said not one of us should
fall by the way; and it was true, for we all
lived to complete our journey and we did not
lose any of our stock. We camped on the Bear
River until more of our company came up,
and we crossed over the river on the 10th of
May.

We continued our journey westward, and
on the 28th of May my wife Sarah M. gave
birth to a little daughter whom we named Eliza
Ann; we camped at the head of the Humboldt
River for a half-day and then traveled on. In
ten days my wife's health was restored to that
degree that she walked a mile without injury,
thus proving to us that our Heavenly Father
was taking care of us and blessing us as
Brigham Young had prophesied to us.

I have ever found that when we are in the
line of our duty and retain our faith in the
promises of God and his inspired servants, we
are watched over by him who holds all things
in his power, and protected from sickness or
evil.

When we reached Gravelly Ford on the
Humboldt, we found the river much swollen
and still rising, so the most of the company
were afraid to cross it that night, but I put all
my family in a large wagon—named the Santa
Fe—which was loaded with salt; then I
hitched twelve yoke of oxen to it, and started
into the water. All went well until we reached
the middle of the stream when the cattle lost

their feet and began to go down stream, while
Brother Jennings and I were trying our best
to turn them back—and James Wrathall, being on one of the lead cattle, was a great help
to us. During this critical time when we were
struggling with the still rising waters and my
family was praying for deliverance from a wa-
tery grave, the rest of the company which we
left on the bank, were encouraging us by continually calling out, "Oh! they are all gone
down;" "they are sinking;" but in spite of
all this we landed safely on the other shore.
Brother Jennings swam back across the river;
we were without bedding or food, but with
our hearts full of thankfulness to our Heavenly Father who had cared for and protected
us on our journey. Some of us were a little fearful about remaining here, as just before our arrival there had been an Indian fight
at this place; but we were unmolested and
in the morning, the river having lowered to
its usual condition, all of the company came
over, bringing everything safely, and we had
a joyful prayer circle again together.

All the way from the Bear River, we had

been somewhat in advance of the rest of the company on account of scarcity of feed. The Indians often came to our camp and would sit around, but we were never molested by them in any way, although it was no uncommon thing to see boards standing at the head of graves telling how many were scalped alive by Indians; and in one place in a canyon there was a notice stating that eight white men were scalped alive and buried in one grave; but He who has ever delivered His Saints in all ages, protected us from harm and danger, and now that we were all together it was a cause of great rejoicing and thanksgiving.

While on this trip we had fresh butter every day as well as all the milk we wanted, for we milked the cows night and morning, then after using what milk we needed, the rest was put in the churn, where by the shaking of the wagon, we had butter before noon. This we all considered a great blessing.

We halted when we reached the Sink of the Humboldt, to rest the cattle, for we had crossed one eighteen-mile desert and also one twenty-six-mile, and now had one which was

forty miles wide. We started in the afternoon and traveled all night, and in the morning just at daybreak the sand was so deep in
places that it drove before the axle of the
wagon; but we had only ten miles of it yet,
and we got through all right, and we rested
again.

We traveled up the Carson River in a southwesterly course until we reached Gold Canyon, where we saw some men washing gold
in tin pans at a creek. The cattle while crossing alkali flats on the Humboldt had drank the
alkali water and a few head belonging to the
rest of the company had died, but according
to the blessing pronounced upon my family
(by Brigham Young), our cattle had come
through safely.

Early in July we arrived in the Washoe Valley, in good health and spirits but glad to find
a resting place.

I bought a place with a house on it, of a
Mr. Samuel Best, and here we stayed, camped
at the foot of the Sierra Nevadas. The
house was a rough affair made of clapboards

but we stayed in it during the day and slept in our wagons at night.

One day while I was away and no one was with the women and children except my father (who was blind) and a hired man, two men came to the camp and demanded supper. They were very wicked looking and the women, with a prayer in their hearts, set out supper for them, which they ate in silence and then said that they wanted their breakfast very early in the morning, and left on their horses in the direction from which they came, towards the creek. All supposed now that they were gone for the night and the men went to bed, but two of the women remained up sewing after putting the rest of the family to bed in the wagons. Suddenly the more evil-looking man who had ordered supper entered the house and in very abusive language asked them "what they were doing there at that time of night."

One of them answered: "We are minding our own business and wish others would do the same."

He then began to abuse Joseph Smith and

the Mormons, using very profane language. Being unable to endure such talk quietly, one of the women, with a silent prayer in her heart, asked:

"Did Joseph Smith or the Mormons ever injure you in any way?"

"No," he answered fiercely. "But I would like to see them all annihilated."

"That you will never live to see," she calmly answered; "and the Lord will hold you responsible for what you have said here tonight."

He sat silent for a few minutes, then quickly arose and left them without a word. After thanking our Heavenly Father for the power which had preserved them from such a man, they gathered all the rest of the family together into one wagon, and one of them kept watch the rest of the night, but the men never came back.

When I returned from California I moved our wagons and family down the Carson Valley about two miles and camped in the cottonwoods near the lake.

Many a night while here in the woods the

Indians would come and cook their squirrels and other meat on our stove, then after they had eaten their supper, they would lie down and sleep all night, leaving in the morning before any of us were up. They never hurt us or molested anything, although one of us would sit up to watch their actions. We had put our trust in our Heavenly Father and to him we offered our prayers for protection and we were preserved by His kind hand.

During the summer I made a number of trips with a train of pack-mules over the Sierra Nevada mountains to "Hang Town," Cal., and back to Carson, thus keeping a store supplied with dry goods and groceries of all kinds.

In the fall I hauled lumber from a saw mill, sixteen miles away, and built a good two-story dwelling house, into which we moved just before winter. We had plenty of good wood to burn, plenty to eat, drink and wear, so we were very comfortable although our neighbors were scarce, the most of the people living at the settlement two miles below us.

In the following spring, 1857, I cut down a number of large pine trees and fenced in about twenty acres; by laying the trees lengthwise along the ground and placing the small end of one on the larger end of another, a fine fence was made to keep out stock.

One day my wife Isabella was going to the home of Geo. Colmer, and while yet in the woods, his dog flew at her and tore several holes in her shoulder and arm. My nephew Abe Layton immediately killed the dog. We kept the wounds bathed in brandy, and put on such poultices as we could get, and the sores healed rapidly.

Grass was plentiful all over the valley. During the summer, I, with the assistance of Wm. Jennings and Wm. Nixon, made a wagon road over the mountains between Hang Town, Cal., and Carson Valley on the old mule trail.

Late in the summer some unknown person set the grass on fire—it was a sight never to be forgotten—sometimes it looked as if the whole valley was in a blaze. For three days all the people turned out and fought the flames.

On August 15, 1857, a little daughter was
born to my wife Caroline C., and we gave her
the name of Selina.

One day, when it was very hot and every
one was busy and the women had forgotten
the children for a few minutes, some one discovered that three of the little ones were miss-
ing. They were Christopher, four years old,
Hyrum, three years, and Polly, only fifteen
months old. The mothers of the little ones
were nearly frantic as there was a large stream
of water running near by, and they called to
the children but no answer came back. All
stopped work and started in search of them,
and finally some one found them under a pine
tree about a mile up the mountain. They
were hurried back to their anxious mothers,
for they had been gone about three hours;
and had crossed a creek, the boys having carried the little girl over. We all gave thanks
to the Lord for thus preserving our little ones.

In September word came to Apostle Orson
Hyde to preach reformation, and accordingly
all the people were rebaptized.

In the fall of 1857, William R. Smith

came with a message from the First Presidency of the Church, stating that the missionaries were recalled to Utah.

Our crops were not all gathered, and some
of our people had sold their cattle to make
improvements on their homes and did not
know how to manage to obey this counsel;
but I arranged to help them with wagons
and mules and provisions.

Brother Thompson had the misfortune to
get his leg broken by a wagon running over
it, and he said:

"For goodness sake, Brother Layton,
don't leave me here."

I assured him that we would not do that,
and then procured a spring wagon for him.

While we were preparing for our return
trip, William R. Smith was sent to buy fire-
arms and ammunition and other supplies for
our journey; but for some unknown reason
he failed to obtain them, so I went and purchased all that we needed for our trip to
Utah.

We left Carson Valley on the 1st day of

10

October, 1857, and the weather was getting quite cool, but we did not mind that.

When we had been traveling a few days several of the little children were taken very sick. One of my little daughters was stricken with the complaint. I immediately administered to her, and her mother doctored her with a little flour and water to which was added a teaspoonful of port wine and one of cinnamon tea, and she soon recovered. Two children in the company died at Stony Point, being the only deaths on the trip.

When we reached Goose Creek mountains a halt was called and all hands turned out and felled the trees to make a new road, to take the wagons up the mountains. While we were doing this the women and children were getting up as best they could. Some of them had a child in one arm, using the other hand to pull them up with, while another little one clung tightly to the mother's skirts. There was snow on the ground, this making it very disagreeable for the climbers; but the Lord gave them strength

and courage to persevere, so that they landed on the other side safely.

Having reached the summit we attached
ropes to the wagons and lowered them down
the other side of the mountains. We drew
into camp and lifted our voices in prayer,
praise and thanksgiving for our safe deliverance from perilous adventures.

The day before we reached Bear River,
October 27, we saw approaching a band of
cavalry and infantry and were much pleased
when they proved to be some of our own
people instead of a portion of Johnston's
army, as at first we had feared.*

When we discovered the soldiers to be
our friends we had a glad, happy time to-

---

*This company, under the command of Chaun-
cey W. West with 600 men, had left Weber county, Utah, on September 23, 1857, by orders from
General Daniel H. Wells, had marched through
Cache, Round and Marsh valleys by forced
marches, and had succeeded in turning the flanks
of the enemy, so they could not enter Utah by the
north, and camped at head of Marsh Valley. Orders came to return by way of Malad Valley. In
crossing the mountain into Malad Valley they
took 7 men (with pack animals) prisoners, and at
Ogden sent them to Salt Lake City.

gether that night. They had two brass bands and by taking turns we had music all night. At daybreak the company were off for Echo Canyon, leaving us cheered, and with renewed strength we went on our way rejoicing.

A stranger near here had told us that the "destroying angels" would be at Bear River and would not let any one cross who had any trouble with their neighbors or the Church, but as we were in accord with the authorities and each other, we were not alarmed by the report.

Arriving at the river the company drew in together for camping, but I, with my family, kept on up the river and never stopped until all our wagons were forded over, it being near ten o'clock when we found a place to camp. We left early in the morning and camped at night near a house where a woman lay dying. The people were very poor, and while my women folks did all they could for the sufferer I left substantial help by adding somewhat to their finances.

We arrived in Kaysville on November 1, 1857, before sundown, having been just a month on the return trip: the rest of the company did not arrive for three days. Brother Thompson came to me and said: "Brother Layton, here is your wagon, for which I shall ever feel grateful." Several ·of the company donated towards the wagon and we gave it to him to keep.

CHAPTER X.

ESTABLISHED IN KAYSVILLE.

Numerous Additions to the Family—Chosen Bishop, also Prominent in Industrial, Political, Military and Pioneering Enterprises.

AFTER staying a few days with William B. Smith (who lived near the lake), I bought a house from David Day (the house where James Green now lives), moved my family there and unloaded the wagons.

I had been here but a short time when I was called to go to Salmon River to bring in the missionaries before spring. This was a hard call to obey, for my children were all small and our provisions for the winter were scarce, and I disliked to leave the women alone; but committing them to the Lord's care and protection, I went where duty called me.

On December 18, 1857, a son was born to

my wife, Isabella G., and we named him Jacob Alonzo.

While I was away Bishop Allen Taylor informed my families that they should get all the wagons and teams in readiness to start on another pilgrimage (they knew not where), so that when I returned I immediately completed the preparations they had commenced.

The weather was very cold, severe and extremely unpleasant.

On the 18th of March, 1858, a son was born to my wife, Sarah M., and we named him Erastus.

In two weeks time, some of my family being ready to move, they went as far as Salt Lake City, and moved into a vacant house belonging to my wife Isabella's father, Brother Richard Golightly, and remained in waiting for the rest of the family. While living here the women made yeast and traded it for flour—which was an expensive article that spring—and in two weeks they took in over two hundred pounds of flour. As soon as the rest of the family arrived, we all started on our journey, and traveling as far as Pelican Point on Utah Lake, found it the roughest place we had ever been (from Kansas to California). I did not like this place at all, for the wind blew a continual sand storm and it was very warm and disagreeable, so I drove on to a grove in American Fork, which was a very pleasant place.

Here we stayed until we had orders to return to our deserted home. Some of us started the next day, while the rest remained two weeks longer, but we were all safely home by the 8th of July. On our exodus south we had left the chickens and domestic animals on the place and now we found them all right, only a little wild. It seemed as if our Heavenly Father had taken care of everything for us that we might have our own on our return. While we were away men had been sent back twice to irrigate the grain and we found it and our potatoes and corn looking fine, most of it ready to harvest—thus our winter's provisions were waiting for the sickle.

On July 11, 1858, a son was born to my wife Sarah B., whom we named Ezra William.

I bought a place on Kays Creek—known as the "prairie house"—and built four large rooms, into which the family moved. We had a large herd of sheep which occupied a great deal of time and gave employment to the older boys. Brother Jennings and I bought about 200 head of freight oxen of Livingston and Kinkead. They were very poor and rundown. We turned them out on pasture and about one-third of them died. The others fattened up and we traded them to the settlers, for cattle or any thing we could get—traded one yoke for two fat hogs; we also kept a butcher shop.

I was ordained a High Priest on February 27, 1859.

In March, 1859, my little son Erastus was taken very sick, and he died on the 20th. My father was also very sick at this time, and when we returned home from Erastus' funeral on the 21st of March we found father dead.

He was buried the next day in the Kaysville cemetery.

The following summer I bought a large train of mules of Beals and Guerney, also some mules of a Mr. C. Crayton.

I loaded the freight teams with flour and freighted to Helena, Montana.

On June 13 a son was born to my wife Caroline, and we gave him the name of James Albert.

In the spring of 1860 I bought a good farm from a man named George Allen, two miles down Kays Creek (now known as the "old farm"), and removed part of my family to it. I had very good crops, hired men and cradled and bound the grain, but as threshing machines were very scarce, was not able to have it threshed until November.

On March 21, 1860, a son was born to my wife Isabella G., and we named him Richard Golightly. In May a daughter was born to my wife Sarah M., whom we named Emma Jane.

During this year there was considerable emigration through Utah, and as I always kept a band of horses, I used to trade my fat horses for their poor ones (many of which after resting and being on pasture awhile, proved to be very good animals. This helped the emigrants to get a good team and also helped me.

On October 17 a son was born to my wife Sarah B., and we named him David Edwin.

In the spring of 1861 I built two new houses and a granary on the farm. I moved the remainder of my family down, then sold the place at Prairie House.

On February 20, a daughter was born to my wife Caroline C., and we named her Martha Alice.

During the summer I helped several poor men to get homes and teams to work with, knowing that the Lord always blesses those who help the poor, for I have proved it many a time.

In July Emma Jane, my little daughter, was taken very ill and died on the 13th.

We had a good crop of grain, so that it required ten men to cradle and bind it.

Utah in 1862 was knocking for admission at the portals of the Federal Union, having completed the telegraph line in the fall of 1861.

On January 6, 1862, mass meetings were held throughout the Territory to elect delegates to the state convention to be held at Salt Lake City on the 20th. I was one of the delegates selected from Davis county to this convention. Despite every favorable indication Utah's efforts for statehood during 1862 failed of success.

On January 24, a daughter was born to my wife, Isabella G., and we gave her the name of Rachel.

At the April Conference I was chosen and set apart as Bishop of the Kaysville ward, Davis county. This necessitated my living in the city, therefore I bought some lots in the city and built a house on them.

On July 3, 1862, a son was born to my wife Sarah M., and we gave him the name of Charles Martin.

That summer I finished the erection of the Kaysville meeting house.

Having two sons now who were large

enough to drive a team, I kept the farm and made some improvements on it; I, with the boys' help, planted an orchard, built a good barn, did a great deal of fencing, and built several stables and sheds for the animals, for I always desired to take good care of everything and not let anything suffer or let anything go to waste.

On August 2, Rosa Ann Hudson and I were married in Salt Lake City, Daniel H. Wells officiating.

On December 8, a son was born to my wife Caroline C.; we named him Heber.

On January 25, 1863, a daughter was born to my wife Sarah B., whom we named Annie Barnes.

That summer, besides making more improvements on the farm, I bought and operated a reaper and mowing machine, which cost $1,000. This being quite a novelty in Utah, a great many people came to see them work. Wheat was $4.00 a bushel. I had planted the first alfalfa seed (on the farm) that was ever planted in Utah, and some of it still grows on the old farm.

In August President Brigham Young and his counselors came and took dinner with us, on their way up to Bear Lake. Our little son, who was a namesake of Heber C. Kimball, was very sick at this time and Brother Kimball blessed him and told his mother that he could not recover, which prophecy came true, for on September 9, his spirit passed away.

On October 21 a son was born to my wife Isabella G., and we called him Samuel.

On November 11 a son was born to my wife, Rosa H., and we named him George Willard.

I gave a large party on Christmas day to all the widows, orphans and the poor of Kaysville over which ward I was presiding, and they seemed to appreciate it very much. We had a very enjoyable time.

On the 1st of January, 1864, my wife Sarah M. was taken sick with a severe pain in her side and breast causing her much distress. Everything that could be done for her relief and comfort was done, but when the disease developed, it proved to be a cancer of the worst kind. In April she requested me to take her to Kaysville, which I did and my wife Caroline tenderly cared for her.

On March 1 I received a certificate of life membership in the Deseret Agricultural and Manufacturing Society of Utah, of which membership I was always proud.

In May President Young sent me an invitation to accompany himself and some of the apostles on a trip to Bear Lake, which I accepted. After my return, Sarah M. grew much worse.

On July 28 a son was born to my wife Caroline C., to whom we gave the name of Joseph.

Death came to the relief of my wife Sarah M. on October 25, 1864. This was a great blow to us all, for in her we lost our best counselor and peacemaker, a true wife and loving mother.

How true it is that

> We live in deeds, not years—
> In thoughts, not breaths—
> In feelings, not in figures
> On a dial.

She was true and faithful to the principles

of the everlasting gospel to the end of her
mortal life, and is gone to await the resurrection of the just, who have gone before her.
May her children emulate her worth to their
latest generation! She was a member of our
Relief Society, in which capacity she was
greatly missed. She was laid to rest in the
Kaysville cemetery. The following verses were
composed by my wife Sarah B. for the conso-
lation of her children:

In this life thy soul was weary,
But now thy spirit is at rest;
And we hope with joy to meet you,
With the assembly of the just.

To us thy memory is ever dear,
Thy kindness stamped upon our hearts;
And we hope with joy to meet you,
Where we never more shall part.

I was very busy with Church duties, and
besides, the work of being Bishop I had much
other business to attend to; nevertheless, with
the help of the Lord and my sons, I improved
the farms on which part of the family lived.
In company with Brother Young I made a trip

to Bear Lake Valley, Idaho, where the Saints were founding new settlements. During this year the Perpetual Emigration Fund company sent 170 wagons, 1,717 oxen, and 277 men to the Missouri River after the immigrants who were too poor to obtain their own transportation.

COPY OF A PATRIARCHAL BLESSING,

Given at Kaysville, February 20, 1865, by John Young, Patriarch, on the head of Christopher Layton, son of Samuel and Isabel Wheeler Layton. Born at Thorncut, Bedfordshire, England, March 8, 1821.

Brother Christopher, I now lay my hands upon your head to bless you. I confirm all former blessings which you have received. You have embraced the gospel of salvation in your youthful days with an honest heart and a full determination to live the life of the righteous and be gathered up with the Saints; choosing rather to suffer affliction with the people of the Lord than to enjoy the pleasures of the world for a season; for you have great respect unto the recompense of your reward.

11

The Lord has had His eye upon you all the days of your life and He has preserved you while the shafts of death have flown on either side, and I feel to bless you in the name of the Lord and say you shall be blessed from this time henceforth and forever, for you desire to do good, therefore good shall be given you: you desire to help build up the kingdom on the earth, therefore you shall be built up. You are a lawful heir to the priesthood which you shall hold a fullness of in the own due time of the Lord. You are of the blood of Israel and one of those who knew the joyful sound of the fullness of the everlasting gospel and the blessings of the fathers, even Abraham, Isaac, and Jacob, shall rest upon your head. You shall be a blessing to your father's house and to your forefathers; you shall be a blessing to all you are associated with. You shall have power to govern and control yourself according to the holy order and honor your holy priesthood, which you shall delight in doing. You shall be a blessing to your family and have power to control all that are under your jurisdiction. You shall have wives and children and a numerous posterity upon the mountains of Israel and they shall be blessed in their generation—and to your increase there shall be no end. You shall have houses and lands, flocks and herds, and the blessings of

the heavens shall be upon your fields and your
gardens and upon your vineyards, for this is
the heritage of the sons of Jacob, and your
name shall be honorable in the midst of the
elders of Israel. As you grow in years you
shall grow in knowledge, and your mind
shall expand to comprehend the great things
of the kingdom of God. The gifts and graces
of the Spirit shall rest upon you and you shall
be filled with wisdom and council and decision
and be quick to comprehend; have power to
officiate in your high and holy calling like a
mighty man of God and be a father to the
fatherless and plead the widow's cause. You
shall have friends upon the right hand and upon
the left, and hold important stations in the
Church of Jesus Christ and be valiant for the
truth. The gifts of the gospel shall rest upon
you and be given unto you and you shall have
power with the heavens and mighty faith in
Jesus and have power to administer in holy
things and to the sick and to the afflicted and
they shall be blest and healed under your ad-
ministration. The spirit of discernment shall
rest upon you, you shall have power to detect
every spirit and be clothed upon with the power of the holy priesthood and your tongue
shall be like the pen of the ready writer and
you may be called by the voice of the Spirit
through His servants to bear your testimony

and your words will be quick and powerful, and the wicked shall tremble before you and the righteous rejoice at the sound of your voice. I seal upon you the blessing of health and life and say the destroyer shall not have power over your tabernacle and no enemy shall have power over you and not a hair of your head shall ever fall by the hand of an enemy, but you shall be preserved on the earth as long as life is sweet unto you. You can live to see the redemption of Zion and be gathered up with the pure in heart. Your ears shall yet hear the sound that Babylon is fallen, for you shall see the downfall of nations and empires and the wonderful works of the Lord in the dispensation in which you live and see Israel gathered and assist in the mighty work. It shall be your meat and drink to do good and help build up the kingdom and all the blessings of the new and everlasting covenant I seal upon your head, and many shall rise up and call you blessed in consequence of your firmness and perseverance in well doing. You shall have power to secure to yourself through your faithfulness an everlasting inheritance in the new heavens and new earth, when all things shall be celestialized. You shall be preserved on earth in your outgoings and incomings and what you put your hands to, shall prosper.

All these blessings I seal upon you because
you are entitled to them, and I say, let your
heart be comforted for your name is written in
heaven and you shall have power to accomplish a great and glorious work on the earth
and lay a sure foundation for a time to come,
which you will by keeping the celestial law,
therefore, celestial blessings shall rest upon
your head. You shall be a savior upon Mount
Zion and have power to gather round you
your posterity, which shall be numerous, and
you shall be associated with the great and the
good. You shall ever have a fullness of joy
and your pathway shall shine brighter and
brighter unto the perfect day and your feet
shall stand upon a sure foundation. You shall
have power to keep hold of the iron rod and
no wicked men or devils shall have dominion
over you. All these blessings are yours upon
condition of your faithfulness and perseverance
and endurance to the end; and I seal upon you
a holy resurrection and say, you shall come
forth clothed upon with your priestly garments
and the power of the holy priesthood to officiate in the great work of the restoration of your
forefathers and stand upon Mount Zion and
have a fullness of joy that you have made
your escape from the pollutions of the world
and that you are numbered among the redeemed. I bless you and say your heart shall

be comforted and you shall have dreams and visions and the angels of mercy shall be with you to buoy you up and give you power and influence and you shall be a mighty man in the Zion of God on the earth. All these blessings I seal upon your head and all that your heart desires in righteousness before your Heavenly Father shall rest upon you, and I do it according to the holy order and sealing power which is committed to the servants of the Lord on the earth to bind for heaven, and say all is yours and you are Christ's, and I say unto you live forever in the name of Jesus. Amen.

(L. A. LITTLEFIELD, reporter.)

On January 7, 1865, Septima Simms and I were married, at Salt Lake City, by Brother Heber C. Kimball.

Attended annual Conference at Salt Lake City and on the 10th of April, a special Conference was held at which we voted to erect a telegraph line through the settlements. About this time there was some trouble with the Indians driving away stock, and some of the Saints were killed and scalped.

Our Territory, as well as the rest of the states and territories, were saddened on April

15 by the news of the assassination of President Lincoln.

In June a treaty was made between the superintendent of the Indian affairs and the principal Indian chiefs, Brigham Young and our leading men being present.

On September 4 my wife Sarah B. gave birth to a daughter whom we called Sarah Elizabeth.

In August I accompanied President Brigham Young and a party of brethren on a missionary trip to Cache Valley.

On November 7 a daughter was born to my wife, Isabella G. and we gave her the name of Lucy Isabella.

President Young issued a circular to the Bishops in the Church, calling upon us to assist in erecting the telegraph line; and I sent teams and men; also furnished many of the poles.

On December 28 a little son was born to my wife, Rosa Ann H., to whom we gave the name of Albert Thomas.

In January, 1866, I bought a large train of freight wagons and mules, and a complete outfit of cooking utensils. This had been a very cold, long winter, but early in the spring I fitted up the best of the wagons and mules, and loaded them with oats for United States horses, gave them into the charge of Henry Foxley, and sent them to Fort Bridger. After they returned and were rested I again loaded the wagons, this time with flour for Montana, where it was worth $16.00 a hundred. My two oldest boys, Christopher and Hyrum, were now 13 and 12 years old, and were very manly and always anxious to do any work well; so I sent them on this trip each, driving a six-mule team, William Galbraith being in charge of the train. In two months they returned safely to us again and the teamsters gave a good account of them. Their mothers and I felt very grateful to the Lord who had brought our boys back to us well and hearty. I put the men to work, some to hauling telegraph poles from the canyon; some hauling rock for the Salt Lake Temple.

On April 12 my wife Caroline C. gave birth to a daughter, to whom we gave the name of Caroline.

On May 19 I was appointed brigade quarter-master of First Brigade, Nauvoo Legion (the militia of Utah Territory), which added somewhat to my other duties.

William Jennings and I built a grist mill in Kaysville, costing about $30,000, which was quite an undertaking at this time with so many other responsibilities. But the mill was a much needed enterprise and proved to be a benefit to the farmers, for we bought grain for cash (money was rather scarce in those days) and I always took delight in helping an honest man to be independent.

In the fall I discharged some of the men who were hauling for me and sold most of the mules and wagons to the settlers around me, and waited for the pay until they could earn it. In this way I helped them to get a start. Of course, sometimes I was imposed upon and lost by trusting them, but the Lord blessed me because I trusted in Him. Many times through life I have seen the fulfillment of the blessing which the Prophet Joseph Smith gave me in Nauvoo.

I sent teams during the winter to haul tith-

ing from the northern settlements to Salt Lake
City.

In August I was elected as a representative
from Davis and Morgan counties to the Legislature of Utah Territory, but it did not con-
vene until December 9.

In January, 1867, the Legislature petitioned
Congress to repeal the anti-polygamy law of
1862, and the General Assembly of Deseret
prayed for admission into the Union as a State.

By the middle of January five hundred miles
of telegraph wire had been stretched, extending from Cache Valley in the north to "Dixie"
in the south. An office had been established
in Kaysville in a store room on my lot opposite the meeting house, with Belle Thompson
as operator (she made her home at my house).
This telegraph had cost $150 a mile.

I was one of those who undertook an expensive work in building a good wagon road
from the mouth of Weber Canyon to Straw-
berry Creek. We built a bridge at the mouth
and had to blast through solid rock in some
places. Two years later the overland railroad
passed over this same road. It was held as a

toll road to defray the expenses. The United States mail also passed over it. On March 1 I received four shares in this Weber Canyon Road Company, representing $200.

In August I was elected again as a representative to the Legislature.

I bought a mule train (of about 20 wagons and 80 mules) from William Crayton who had just returned from California, and loaded these with flour for Fort Bridger; then after they returned I sent them to southern California for a quartz mill, which I sent to Helena, Montana.

I attended the October Conference, which was the first meeting held in the large Tabernacle, during which Conference Joseph F. Smith was chosen to fill the vacancy in the Council of the Twelve Apostles caused by the apostasy of Amasa M. Lyman.

At this Conference also 183 missionaries were called to go with their families and strengthen the settlements in southern Utah.

This was the origin of the famous "Muddy Mission"—which was afterwards abandoned because it was in Nevada and because of the unhealthy climate. I, being much interested in this move, helped all I could with outfits, etc.; furnished one family with teams, wagon and all else necessary for the trip.

On November 2 a little son was born to my wife, Rosa Ann H., and we named him Heber Chase.

On November 21 the first number of the *Deseret Evening News* was issued in Salt Lake City with Geo. Q. Cannon as editor, which publication I have taken ever since.

On December 24 I had the brass band come to our house and my wife Caroline gave them an excellent supper, and we all had an enjoyable time. After they were gone and we were settling down for the night, my wife Septima S. presented us with a little daughter, whom we named Amy Caroline.

On January 13, 1868, the Utah Legislature convened. During its session the word "Great" was dropped from both Salt Lake and the City; Richland county was changed to Rich county, and Morgan City was incorporated. While in Salt Lake City I made my home with

Sister Rachel Grant (the mother of Apostle Heber J. Grant).

On January 21 a son was born to my wife, Caroline C., to whom we gave the name of Frank Gunnell.

Attended annual Conference in Salt Lake City in April, and found on returning that my wife, Isabella G., had given birth, on April 9, to a daughter. We named her Jane.

In June I attended a mass meeting at Salt Lake, called by President Young, in which we passed resolutions to assist the Union Pacific and Central Pacific Railroads through the Territory and also to construct a branch road from Ogden to Salt Lake City called the Utah Central, of which I was elected a director.

Attended the funeral of Heber C. Kimball, first counselor to Brigham Young, at Salt Lake City, on June 24.

This year the grasshoppers came in droves and ate up our crops, which was quite discouraging; but we put our trust in the Lord and He sent the sea-gulls to rid us of the pests, and we were very thankful for our deliverance.

On October 16 Zion's Co-operative Mercantile Institution commenced operations in Salt Lake City, with Brother Brigham as its president. Shortly afterwards, "co-op." stores were opened in most of the settlements. I had one started in Kaysville as I was one of the directors.

CHAPTER XI.

YEARS OF EMPIRE-BUILDING.

Dry Farming on the "Ridge"—Railroading and
Merchandising—Perilous Trip on Salt Lake—
Happy and Prosperous Years.

IN the spring of 1869 I took up land north
of Kaysville (known as the range or sand
ridge). Some of my intimate friends asked
me if I had gone crazy to imagine I could
farm that sandy desert. Others told me it was
simply ridiculous, I would only waste my time
and lose my seed grain. To be sure, the wind
at times was terrible and the sand cut off and
destroyed much of the grain, but I never believed in giving up easily, and I persevered
until I made a success of it, and today it blossoms as the rose, and is covered with many
comfortable homes, surrounded by lovely or-

chards, good gardens, fine pastures, hay and grain lands.

May 17 the first ground was broken by President Young for the building of the U. C. R. R. The weather was bright and beautiful, and a great many leading people were present. After speaking and other ceremonies the assembly dispersed while the band played a martial air.

No large contracts were let in the building of this line, which was literally constructed by our people who, for pay, took stock in the road. I was one of the first to take contracts by which I furnished timbers for bridges and trestle work, etc.

On June 20 I accompanied President Young and other brethren to Bear Lake Valley, where the Saints were organized into a stake, with David P. Kimball as president.

On August 25 a son was born to my wife, Rosa Ann H., and we gave him the name of Ernest.

In the fall I built a large white house with granite corners near the grist mill in Kaysville. I now owned eight houses here. Being desirous that my children should attend a good school, I moved one of my families to Salt Lake City that they might have educational advantages.

On January 10, 1870, the last spike in the Utah Central Railroad was driven by President Young at the depot grounds in Salt Lake City. It had been now eight months since this road was commenced. The weather was cold and frosty, the sun being behind a fog or cloud for the most of the day. A little after noon three guns were fired, which was a signal for the raising of flags throughout the city and the assembling of the people to witness the ceremony. Before 2 o'clock the train bringing invited guests from Ogden and the north came up to the end of the track amidst the cheers of the assembled multitude of fully 15,000 people.

Seated on an open platform car overlooking the scene were the president, general superintendent and other officers and directors, I among the latter, also representatives from the Union and Central Pacific, and other prominent men. Just about 2 p. m. the sun burst through the mists which had hitherto obscured it and it

12

shone brilliantly upon the driving of the last spike by President Young with an elegantly chased steel mallet made for this occasion at the Church blacksmith shops; the spike was also of home-made iron.

After the ceremony a salute of 37 guns was fired—one for each mile of road. We had music furnished by the bands of Captain Croxall, Camp Douglas and Tenth Ward, at intervals during the afternoon; also speeches by many prominent officials and men of distinction; some addresses were omitted because of the coldness of the weather. All spoke of the fact that this road was the only one built without government subsidies; for every shovelful of dirt had been removed by the working men of Utah, and every bar of iron of the road had been placed in position by their labor. We thus owned our own road. We were advised not to stop where we were for as the last two rails stuck out a little, that meant "go on."

At night the city was brilliantly illuminated and fireworks were in various parts of the city; we had a magnificent display on Arsenal Hill. A grand ball and supper at the Theater, attended by leading Church officials, prominent merchants, both Mormon and Gentile, officers from Camp Douglas, and many citizens, made a fitting finale for the day's memorable proceedings.

Our days of isolation were now forever past and with our steam and electrical communications we could stand face to face with all the good and evil that modern civilization represents.

On the following night another dance and supper was given for the invited guests in the city, and on the next night we had a grand dance and excellent supper for those who had worked on the railroad. All of my children who were old enough went to this ball and had a most enjoyable time.

On January 13 a mass meeting was held in Kaysville (and also in most of the Utah settlements) at which the ladies protested against the passage of the Cullom anti-polygamy bill, introduced in Congress.

On January 19 a daughter was born to my wife Septima S. and we gave her the name of Priscilla May.

On February 12 an act was passed by the legislature by which the women of Utah were granted the elective franchise.

On May 1 Mary Jane Roberts and I were married in Salt Lake City, by Daniel H. Wells.

Attended the funeral of Patriarch John Young; also the annual Conference held on May 5 to 8.

This summer the grasshoppers did much damage all through the Territory, and I spent much of my time in looking after my farming interests.

Attended the three days' discussion between Orson Pratt and Dr. John P. Newman on the question, "Does the Bible sanction Polygamy?" In August, Martin Harris, then aged 88 years, came to Salt Lake City, and at the Conference I heard him bear a faithful testimony to the truth of the Book of Mormon, of which he was one of the Witnesses.

On September 10 our household was visited by the death angel who took the spirit of my son Frank Gunnell, son of my wife Caroline. We buried him in Kaysville cemetery.

The surviving members of Zion's Camp and

the Mormon Battalion had a very enjoyable party at the Social Hall in the city on October 10, at which 32 of Zion's Camp and 63 of the Battalion boys were present.

My sons were now a great help to me, for they were trusty boys and very obedient. l always tried to be a kind and affectionate father and maintain my place as the head of my family and they loved to obey me and seemed to regard my word as law to them. The Lord prospered me and I always felt to acknowledge his hand in all things. He blessed me many times with a far-seeing eye that I might make calculations for the maintenance of my wives and children and I always exhorted them to thank God for all His blessings to us.

The Utah Southern R. R. Company was organized January 17, 1871, of which I became one of the stockholders; the ground was not broken for this road till the 1st of May, and it was completed in September.

In the spring William Galbraith and I bought a saw mill of Apostle John Taylor, situated in the east fork of Taylor Canyon. In less than a year we moved it to Arbuckle Canyon. I bought out Galbraith, took R. W. Burton and William Beasley as partners and moved it back to the west fork of Taylor Canyon. I kept about 20 men at work, and as cooks were very unsatisfactory, my wife, Rosa A. H., did our cooking: we sawed from 7,000 to 10,000 feet of lumber a day; and sold most of it to the railroad company. I ran this sawmill until the fall of 1873, when I sold it to Robert Burton.

August 3, 1871, a daughter was born to my wife, Mary R., and we gave her the name of Florence; and on November 1 my wife Rosa A. H. gave birth to a son, whom we called Isaac Clarence.

This year several hundred stands of Italian bees were brought into the Territory, and I bought three stands from a man named Putman. The stands had an inside glass door and it was a great enjoyment to watch the little bees while at work.

On January 27, 1872, a son was born to my wife Caroline C., and we gave him the name of Frederick C.

The Utah Legislature again passed a resolution for the election of delegates to adopt a State constitution; and asked for the admission of Utah into the Union.

On March 23 a little daughter came to my wife, Septima S., and we named her Drucilla Grace.

Court proceedings were still being continued against all of our leading men.

Attended April Conference. In the spring of this year President Young asked me to take a herd of Church sheep, 5,000 in number, which I accepted. I went to Corinne, Box Elder county, and purchased a steam tug-boat (then known as the "Kate Conner"), and some flat-bottomed scows; attached these to "Kate Conner" and towed them to a point near Black Rock, near Salt Lake City, shipped the sheep over to Antelope Island (also called Church Island), then shipped about 2,000 of my own sheep over, thus making 7,000 in all. This business I placed in the hands of my older sons and some other young men. In order to fence properly, we were obliged to make several trips to the Promontory for cedar posts, and in some of these trips we encountered severe storms. On one occasion we were returning from the Promontory, towing the scows loaded with timber and posts. It was oppressively hot and not a breeze stirring, when suddenly the wind commenced blowing and it increased in violence until the water was lashed into white-capped waves, the boat rocked from side to side and the flat boats dragged and held the steamer down till the water ran over the deck at every plunge. Thinking it would be safer for the boat if the scows were astern, we loosened the ropes from the wheelhouses (the steamer was a side-wheeler), and attached them to the stern.

During this change while the boat was reeling from the force of the storm, a rope caught my son Hyrum's foot and dragged it into the paddles of the wheel, crushing it badly, and crippling him for several months.

We now cast anchor but this only caused the water to flow over the deck in a worse manner, so we cut the flat boats loose just before sundown. The engineer at the first approach of the storm had deserted his post, and crawling into his bunk, had covered his head and lay there shivering from fear, helpless and much to be pitied. With our fuel gone and our engineer frightened nearly to death, our boat pitching in all directions, we could not sleep but watched anxiously all night. Sometimes we would sing a hymn, and often we united in prayer, for I felt that our Heavenly Father alone could save us.

About daylight the anchor-cable broke and we were adrift and at the mercy of the furious waves and wind. I thought we must get up steam and try to control the boat, so I spoke to the engineer, but with a shiver he answered: "The fire is out—the wood-boats are gone—oh—I can't start a fire—oh—oh." Leaving him to his despair, we emptied our coal oil on some cotton waste and soon had a roaring fire, but in order to keep it going we were obliged to burn anything we could. We burned barrels, tables, chairs, for I thought I could get another boat but not another set of boys like these. So with two at the pilot wheel and taking turns at engineering, with the help of the Lord we kept the boat right side up and landed safely.

I had charge of the sheep and island for
five years and we had many exciting adventures and also some accidents, but no lives were
lost and many are the good pleasant times we
had.   At shearing-time our girls and boys,
with one of my wives to take charge of affairs,
would go over to the island.   Also at haying
time the young folks enjoyed the pleasure of
these trips.

On one occasion we were bringing a load
of fat sheep to Salt Lake for mutton, when
the boat was caught in the floating ice, which,
coming from Bear River and Jordan River,
had met and formed a "jam," from which we
were unable to extricate ourselves for 48 hours.
The pounding of the ice on the sides of our
boat caused it to leak.   We all united in calling upon the Lord in our extremity, and my
wives and children who were on shore and
could see our peril, also prayed for help.   A
wind arose which drove the ice away so we
were enabled to reach shore, although we
were obliged to go back to the island first,
then the next morning the ice being gone we
easily crossed and were received with much re-

joicing by those dear ones who had been so anxious for our safety.

A great deal of my wool was taken to the Co-op. Woolen Factory at Brigham City, where it was exchanged for flannel for dresses, jeans for boys' clothes, linsey for sheets, yarn for stockings, etc. This mill in 1877 was burned down but in less than six months was rebuilt.

In the summer I moved part of the family to the saw mill. Several of my boys had now reached manhood, and as they were honest and industrious, I could trust them with various branches of my business, and they were always loyal to my will. I also was blessed with good sons-in-law and they could always be depended on, which was a great help to me.

In June the First Presidency issued a circular, calling on the people to raise money to bring poor Saints to Utah. The sum of $14,000 was raised.

William Jennings and I built a grist mill at Kaysville, and Thos. Bayanton was our miller, while my son Christopher was receiver and bookkeeper.

In the fall I resigned my position as director

of the railroad, for my duties were many and kept a great many young men employed in various ways, for whenever I found a man trying to help himself I employed him at something, but I always despised an idler.

PATRIARCHAL BLESSING,

By C. W. Hyde, Patriarch, upon the head of Christopher, son of Samuel Layton and Isabella Wheeler, born at Thorncut, Bedfordshire, England, on March 8, 1821.

Dear Brother Layton, I place my hands upon your head and seal upon you a father's blessing which shall be sealed and recorded in the book of life for your good; and great shall be thy wisdom and knowledge before the Lord thy God, and inasmuch as thou shalt be humble, the Lord shall give thee great wisdom that no one shall excel thee; thou shalt have counsel and wisdom from on high and the spirit of prophecy shall be given to comprehend the mysteries of the kingdom of God, for thou art a descendant of Joseph and a lawful heir to the fullness of the priesthood, and wives, and a great kingdom upon the earth; thou shalt lead many to Zion with songs of everlasting joy, and thine inheritance shall be beautiful and thou shalt converse with many of the holy prophets and help to redeem the dead till thou art satisfied. It is thy privilege to stand upon the earth till the coming of the Messiah. Thou shalt sit in council with the general assembly of the First-born, and shalt partake of all her glories and reign as king of kings and be crowned with eternal lives to God and the Lamb forever and ever. Amen.

Kaysville, November 24, 1872.

Early in the spring of 1873 President Brigham Young called a number of missionaries from different parts of the Territory to plant colonies in Arizona. Of these, nine young men, E. C. Phillips, Joseph Robbins, Elijah Laycock, John Seaman, Joseph Woolley, Joseph Adams, William Smith, William Duffin and Ed Bodley, were called from Kaysville, and on March 8 all met in Salt Lake City at the Tabernacle to receive instructions from the authorities. Soon after they started southward in organized companies.

They arrived at the Little Colorado River May 22, after an arduous journey; by May 28 the river was dry and word was sent to

President Young of the barrenness of the country, and the many obstacles to be overcome; and on July 22 they were recalled to Utah, having gained nothing but experience.

My daughters, as well as my sons, were now able to help; one—Eliza Ann M.—taught school, and one—Selina C.—manipulated the telegraph instrument at Kaysville—also taught the younger girls.

Salt Lake City was first lighted by gas during this summer.

This year I began taking up land on what was known as the "Big Range" and determined to thoroughly try "dry-farming" which was a new experience in this place; and many people in Kaysville and Davis county today thank me for making a success of it.

On October 8, a daughter was born to my wife, Mary J. R., and we named her Ella.

On November 17 my daughter Selina C. was married to Edward C. Phillips, by Daniel H. Wells, at Salt Lake City.

Attended a grand celebration at Provo, November 25, on the event of the Utah Southern Railway being completed to that city.

On December 8 my daughter, Eliza Ann
M., was married to Joseph G. Allred; also my
son, Hyrum John, was married to Mary L.
Egbert, Daniel H. Wells officiating at both
ceremonies. In the evening we had a nice re-
ception at Brother Egbert's residence. Thus
the year closed joyously and happily.

During the year 1874 the Utah Northern
Railway was opened from Ogden to Franklin,
Idaho. There was a general religious move-
ment among the Lamanites, hundreds of Indians being baptized into the Church.

On January 18 my son Christopher was married to Jane Bodley, by Daniel H. Wells, in
Salt Lake City.

My wife Rosa Ann H. presented me with a
daughter on February 2, whom we named
Mary Isabell.

Senator Geo. Q. Cannon presented a memorial to Congress on March 2, asking for Statehood, but was again denied.

In April 1 a box containing valuable records
was deposited in the wall of the St. George
Temple and work was pushed towards its completion with all possible speed.

On May 3, George D. Watt of Kaysville
was excommunicated from the Church for
apostasy.

I went down to Salt Lake City on the 6th
of May, and early on the morning of the 7th a
little son came to my wife, Caroline C. We
named him Chauncey West. Conference convened at 10 o'clock and continued till the 10th.
The principal subject was the "United Order"
which was organized with Brigham Young
as president.

On May 12 my wife, Septima S., gave birth
to a little son, whom we called Oscar George.

This summer was remarkable for much light-
ning, thunder and rain storms.

Pioneer Day was celebrated by a grand ju-
venile jubilee in the large Tabernacle at Salt
Lake City, at which time 4,000 Sunday School
children did the singing.

Besides my duties as Bishop I farmed over
200 acres, ran the saw-mill and grist-mill and
had the care of from 7,000 to 8,000 sheep.
This kept my sons and sons-in-law employed:
neither were my daughters idle, for some of

them taught school, others were in the telegraph offices and all of them did their own
dressmaking. We all worked together in unity
as one family, and always stood by each other
under all circumstances. If one had a trial or
disappointment we all sympathized, or if one
had a blessing or pleasure, we all rejoiced together. I love now to recall the many social
chats we often had, when I would tell them
of my early life, how I had managed to get
along; advise them how they could help themselves through life; how ready they all were
to accept my counsel and act upon it. These
were very happy years although the responsibilities of my position, as a father and a Bishop, were great and manifold. I feel to praise
the Lord that He has allowed me to see my
children grow up honest, straightforward and
industrious; willing to make sacrifices if need
be for their religion's sake.

In October the Agricultural and Manufacturing Association held a fair at Salt Lake
City, at which I entered a number of sheep,
cows, calves, and a Durham bull. I received
two diplomas for finest sheep; also diploma for

12

Durham cow—Annie—and her calf. The award for best Durham bull was a silver cup, gold lined, which was given me. I gave my wife Rosa H. my diploma for the cow and calf, my diploma for best bucks to my daughter Eliza A. M., and my diploma for best ewes to my daughter Selina C.

On November 5 we had the pleasure of welcoming my brother, John Layton, and his daughter, Mary Ann, to our home. They had left England with 155 other Saints under the direction of William N. Fife, on the steamship "Wyoming," on September 14.

March 25, 1875, the founder of Kaysville, William Kay, died at Ogden, and a large crowd of us went up to the funeral.

In April the trial of Geo. Reynolds for polygamy was commenced. This was a test case and was watched closely by all. When he was sentenced to imprisonment the case was appealed and he was granted bail for $10,000.

This spring I bought a flour mill at Payson, Utah county. I obtained a good miller and sent my son William to take charge of it, but it was so far away from home that I did not keep it very long, but sold it for a good price in about a year.

Having a large family of my own to provide for, and keeping so many men employed, whose families needed supplies, I thought it better to buy goods by wholesale, so I built a large mercantile house and ran that business for a number of years.

On June 10, the first Young Men's Mutual Improvement Association was organized and the work was made universal throughout all the settlements of Saints.

On June 12, my wife Rosa Ann H. gave birth to a daughter, and we named her Jeanetta.

On July 10 Martin Harris, one of the Three Witnesses to the Book of Mormon, died at Clarkston, Cache county, being 92 years old.

On July 17 President Brigham Young, his counselors and many others renewed their covenants by baptism, and this example was followed by the Saints generally. Every one of my family over eight years old renewed their covenants in this way.

In September I attended the funeral, at Salt

Lake City, of George A. Smith, President Young's counselor.

I moved the Church sheep from the island into Southern Utah for the winter to a place called Cove Fort.

At a meeting of the stockholders of the Zion's Co-operative Mercantile Institution, held at Salt Lake City on October 5, I was duly elected to the office of director of said institution, which position I held for a year.

At the October conference, the Tabernacle was dedicated, and a great number of missionaries were called.

In December the ladies of Utah sent a petition to Congress with 23,626 signatures, asking for Statehood and the repeal of the antipolygamy laws.

On December 28 a son was born to my wife, Mary J. R., and we named him Levi Brigham.

The year 1876 was noted for the settlements of Saints in lower Utah, Arizona and Mexico. In February a number of missionaries were called to go to Arizona, my son Hyrum among them. They traveled by teams and on March

21 arrived at Little Colorado, and founded colonies.

In April the new Z. C. M. I. building on Main St., Salt Lake City, was opened for business.

I attended the annual Conference from April 6 to April 10.*

On May 16, 1876, the Y. L. M. I. A. was organized at Kaysville with Ada Williams as president, Eliza A. Allred; first counselor, and Helen Hyde, second counselor, Mary Ann

---

*"A disaster of an exceptional nature occurred at Salt Lake City the' day before the opening of this conference. It was the explosion of 40 tons of blasting and gunpowder, stored in four stone magazines located on Arsenal Hill. About 5 o'clock in the afternoon, every one was startled by two terrific reports, almost simultaneously; after the lapse of a few seconds, two other convulsions followed equally deafening. In a moment missiles whistled and tore through the air over almost the entire city, while houses tottered and trembled, roofs, walls and ceilings were rent, windows smashed and hundreds of persons prostrated on the ground. Dense volumes of smoke hovered over the spot, thus indicating what had happened. The explosion was distinctly heard and felt at Farmington, 15 miles north, and even caused the vibration of buildings at Kaysville, 5 miles further."—Whitney's History of Utah.

Layton, secretary, and Selina Layton Phillips, assistant secretary.

The sheep which I had taken into Southern Utah had fared badly during the winter, and I returned them back to the Church; in order to return the proper number I was obliged to make up losses from my own herd and consequently I had very few left. This was quite a loss to me, but I would not let the Church property suffer.

In June the case of George Reynolds was again argued on appeal before the supreme court of the Territory, and in July the case was again appealed to the supreme court of the United States.

At the Conference in October, John W. Young, son of the President, was sustained as first counselor, in place of George A. Smith.

On October 7 my wife Septima S. gave birth to a son, whom we named Harry Wilford.

The Brigham Young Academy was founded on October 16 at Provo.

On October 26 a son was born to my wife, Caroline C., and we gave him the name of Horace.

This fall I bought a thorough bred Norman stallion and ten mares from Logan and Wilson of Missouri, and raised some of the finest stock in the Territory. I also oversaw the planting and harvesting of the largest amount of small grain ever raised in Utah. I was one of the first to cut grain with a header. This grain was raised on the Sand Ridge by what was known as dry farming.

I kept on buying more arid land until my sons and I owned about a thousand acres. We also owned three headers and a thresher and other machinery for this work.

I distributed dry farm grain throughout the county and assisted men to take up this dry land and to raise grain, for I told them that "where there is good sagebrush, grain will grow."

On March 4, 1877, my daughter, Martha Alice C., was married to James T. Walker, at Salt Lake City, Daniel H. Wells officiating.

In the later part of March, Apostle Joseph F. Smith and wife, my wife Mary J. R. and I, in company with Presidents Young and Wells, some of the apostles and leading elders, started

by team for St. George to attend Conference
and dedicate the Temple at that place.

Conference convened on April 6 continuing
three days. President Young addressed the
Conference at five of the six meetings, dilating
upon the duties of all officers, urging them to
faithfully perform the sacred tasks allotted
them. The second day of conference President Young took the initial step of the important work of more thoroughly organizing the
stakes of Zion, first setting in order the St.
George stake, and after that the others
throughout the Church. A number of missionaries were also called. On the return trip
Brother Brigham and his counselors stopped
at Manti, Sanpete Co., and dedicated a Temple site, Brother Young offering the prayer
and breaking the ground for the foundation.
Through Beaver our party was accompanied
by a guard of about twenty-five young men,
who deemed this precaution necessary because
of threats said to have been made against the
President's life by some of the relatives or
sympathizers of John D. Lee, who had recently been executed. Brother Young gave us in-

structions in our duty of training and educating our children to lives of purity and usefulness, and urged co-operative action in all our temporal interests.

On May 18 the ground for the Logan Temple was dedicated, Apostle Orson Pratt offering the prayer.

About this time a survey was made for a canal, which was called "Weber and Davis Co.'s Canal." I was one of the stockholders, and put a number of men and teams to work on it. I sold some of the teams and let the men work it out in contracts on the canal, taking stock, thus their paying terms were easy and I became a larger stockholder.

CHAPTER XII.

LAST YEARS IN KAYSVILLE.

In Stake Presidency—Death of Brigham Young—
Family Marriages, Births and Deaths—Forced
into Hiding to Escape Persecution—Called to
Arizona.

A T a special conference at Farmington, on
June 17, 1877, a stake was organized in
Davis county, with Wm. R. Smith, of Center-
ville, as president, and myself of Kaysville,
and Anson Call of Bountiful as his counselors.
As I was now released from my office of Bishop, Brother Peter Barton was chosen in my
place.

Zion was extending its borders in all directions, settlements were growing larger, and
many new wards were being formed, among
which was South Hooper, (which had been a
part of Kaysville) with Henry B. Gwilliams
as Bishop.

In July Brother Brigham Young deeded
9642 acres of land in Cache Valley to the Brigham Young Academy at Logan.

On August 23 our President was taken suddenly sick with cholera morbus, and about four o'clock in the afternoon of August 29 the immortal spirit of Brother Brigham passed from the earth. A profound sorrow rested like a pall upon the Saints all over the world when it became known that our loved and honored leader was no more; as Israel mourned for Moses, so we mourned in heartfelt sorrow for Brother Young.*

---

*"The coffin containing his body was encased in a metallic covering in which was inserted a plate glass of sufficient size to admit of a view of the departed. It was tastefully draped with white and wreathed with flowers. At 10:30 a. m. the gates of the Temple Block were thrown open, and the crowds of anxious people who had gathered, gained ingress to the Tabernacle. For the next twenty-five hours—the building being kept open all night—a continuous stream of living humanity passed through, nearly twenty-five thousand people taking a farewell look at the face of the dead. On the Sabbath, September 2, the family of the deceased, his counselors, the apostles and other officers of the Priesthood, with the general public, listened to the speakers who addressed them, expressing the sentiments of sorrow that pervaded the hearts of the Saints, yet exhibited a calm resignation to the Divine will. The building was filled, all available standing room in aisles and doorways being taken up. The procession moved to the private cemetery, where the body was placed

On the 4th of September the apostles publicly assumed their position as head of the Church, the Saints returned to their duties and everything was again in working order.

About this time I took a trip across the country to St. Louis, Mo., where I purchased a carload of large mules, which I brought back to Utah, and used to great advantage on my dry farm lands.

In November a company of Saints from Utah arrived on the San Pedro river, in Arizona and founded the settlement of St. David.

My wife, Isabella G., who had been sick for a long time, left us to mourn her loss, on December 15. She had always been greatly loved in the family and was a general favorite, and her children—three girls and four boys— were welcomed and well cared for by my other wives. Her disease was dropsy. She had

---

in the vault prepared for it. The grave was dedicated by Apostle Wilford Woodruff. Among the mighty ones of earth shall be the name of him of whom it has been written:
"He loved his people: their high destiny
Will be a monument to Brigham Young."
—Whitney's Hist. of Utah.

also been a Relief Society teacher for several years.

On December 28 a little daughter came to my wife, Mary J. R., and we called her Harriet Ann.

On January 10, 1878, my son, Ezra William, was married to Mary Ellen Colmer in Salt Lake City.

Attended Conference at Salt Lake City from April 6th to the 8th.

This summer I was busy with my mercantile business, milling work and farming.

On August 15, 1878, I was married to Elizabeth Williams in the Endowment House at Salt Lake City, Joseph F. Smith officiating.

In the fall I bought a band of horses of William H. Hooper, giving $10,000 for them. I sold half of them—320 head—afterwards to William R. Smith, also 80 head to William Stokes, besides many teams to different men.

On December 12 my daughter Mary Ann was married to George Swan, Jr., in Salt Lake City, by Daniel H. Wells; and on the same day my wife Rosa Ann presented me with a daughter, whom we named Rozina.

On January 6, 1879, the supreme court of
the United States unanimously affirmed the
constitutionality of the anti-bigamy law of
1862, and confirmed the sentence of the lower
courts upon George Reynolds.

My son, John H., was married on January
23, to Hannah Phillips at Salt Lake City by
Daniel H. Wells.

On February 20 I attended the trial of Robert T. Burton on a charge of murder committed during the Morrisite difficulty of 1862.
A verdict of not guilty was rendered on
March 7.

A little son came to my wife, Septima S., on
March 21, and we named him Franklin Simms.

This spring I built a large frame house on
the Sand Ridge, which we called the Summit
farm and dug the first well, going one hundred feet, and after digging several we got a
good one with plenty of water. Before this
we had to haul the water in a iron tank holding 560 gallons.

At the annual Conference this year the main
business was the calling of a number of elders
for foreign missions, and Brother Moses

Thatcher was chosen to fill the vacancy in the Twelve Apostles, caused by the death of Orson Hyde.

On April 24 the first Utah wheat was shipped by ocean to Liverpool, England, from San Francisco, in the sailing vessel "Ivy," by S. W. Sears, and I often wondered how many of my old friends and relatives ate bread made from our wheat.

Emma Smith, formerly wife of the Prophet Joseph Smith, died at her home in Nauvoo, Illinois, April 30.

On the 6th of May there was a grand demonstration in honor of Daniel H. Wells, who had been released from the territorial penitentiary, where he had been sent three days before by Judge Emerson for alleged contempt of court, because he had refused to describe the endowment clothing.

On August 4 my wife Elizabeth W. gave birth to a little son, whom we called Lawrence, but after a few weeks he was recalled to his heavenly home, and on August 28 his spirit fled from us.

I was made president of the Farmer's Union,

which institution I founded in Layton, and held that position a number of years.

On September 26, my wife Caroline C. gave birth to a little son, whom she called Benjamin; and on September 28 we were called to mourn the death of baby Franklin S., the son of my wife Septima.

About the first of November I made a trip to San Francisco, Cal., accompanied by my wife Lizzie.

During the next two or three years—1880-1883—although I had broken no law of God or man, it became necessary for my personal safety that I should be in hiding from those who were so strenuously making arrests under the Edmunds-Tucker law.

Finally my wives and children agreed that, although they disliked very much to be without my presence, yet they would rather know that I was at liberty than to have me dodging the hounds of the law, and under these conditions, I accepted a call to preside over, and make a home for, Saints in Southern Arizona.

CHAPTER XIII.

PRESIDING IN ARIZONA.

Fifteen Years of Great Activity and Success—
The Enemy Also Busy—Many New Enter-
prises Established—Leader,   Adviser   and
Father to the Colonists.

IN February, 1883, I was set apart in Salt
Lake City as President of the St. Joseph
stake in Arizona, and I immediately began to
make preparations to leave for that territory.
I chartered two cars and loaded them with
horses, mules, furniture, farm implements,
seeds, alfalfa, oats, wheat and flour enough to
last a year. By the 15th we were ready to
start.

Our party consisted of my wife Lizzie and
two children, her sister Fannie and brother
Henry; my sons Richard, Joseph and William; my nephew, Charles Layton, and wife;

14

also Dave Gaily, Geo. Steed and Thomas
White.

Arriving at St. David on Saturday, Feb.
24, we went directly to David P. Kimball's
house, and on Sunday, the 25th, at the meeting of the Saints in St. David, they sustained
me as president of the stake with David P.
Kimball as first and James H. Martineau as
second counselors.

On Feb. 28 the boys of our party came
in with the stock, furniture, etc., which had
traveled slower than we.

After staying a few days at Brother Kimball's I moved the family into the Campbell
mill building where we remained about three
weeks. Then I moved to a Mexican grant
where we lived in tents and had our cook-
stove under a tree; but I did not stay here
very long as we were obliged to haul water
over three miles.

The first week in March a party of nine,
with a four-horse team and a single team,
started on a general exploration trip to see the
country. They went to Tombstone the first
night: then through the Sulphur Springs Val-

ley, which they thought was the finest stock range they had ever seen (except Cache Valley, Utah); then through the Gila Valley, which place I particularly desired them to visit. Their report of this section was very favorable—more settlers than when I was there. They were gone about three weeks.

On March 23 my daughters Eliza A. Allred and Drucilla Grace Layton came from Utah and my son-in-law Joseph G. Allred arrived on the 25th with another car, containing potatoes, barbwire, iron posts, some machinery, also chickens, which we turned loose, and of course they soon found their own roosts.

I took my wife and daughters three miles down the San Pedro River to see a place called the Merrimont ranch and as there were about thirty-seven springs on the place everything looked green and bright, although there was only one tree (a juniper) in the vicinity. The women were much pleased with the locality and exclaimed joyously, "This is the prettiest place we have seen in the country." I bought this ranch, but the wind blew so hard every day we could not live in tents, there-

fore I went to work building a house and also
bought the Campbell mill house and had it
moved on to the ranch. My women folks became quite lonesome, discouraged and home-
sick at times, although they tried to be cheerful, and I consoled them by telling of our
blessings and showing them that our heavenly
Father was very kind and merciful to us because things might have been a great deal
worse.

I, with the boys' help, fenced in 320 acres
and made a canal for two miles. One afternoon we missed the horses and we all started
out in different directions to hunt them, but
not finding them, came back at night, except
Richard and Joseph Allred, who had followed
tracks leading toward Tucson. About ten
o'clock that night they stopped at Pantana
Seneca; in the morning they met a man who
had seen the horses and after some conversation said he would get them, so the boys
came back home. The next day the man
brought five horses—one out of each team—
and received his reward. After a few days

we found one at Benson, but it was a year
before we found all of them.

We plowed 100 acres, put in alfalfa, wheat
and oats, and had just finished when rains
commenced. The grain started fine and we
were much rejoiced; then rain ceased and
consequently the crops burned up.

I attended Conference at Salt Lake City on
April 6, and my son William's wife and two
children came with me when I returned to
Arizona.

In May I went over to the Gila River and
held a two days' meeting at Pima; on the
13th organized the Saints into four wards,
namely: Pima, with Joseph K. Rogers, Bishop; Thatcher, John M. Moody, Bishop; Graham, Jorgen Jorgenson, Bishop; Curtis (now
Eden), Moses Curtis, Bishop.

On June 27th my son Wm. Layton was
chosen first counselor to Bishop Wm. D.
Johnson of St. David ward.

Conference was held at St. David on June
2 and 3, at which the Relief Society was organized with Sister Wilmuth East as presi-

dent, Sister Cyrena Merrill as first and Sister Mary Ransom as second counselors.

During the summer all of us had chills and fever except myself, sometimes three or four of us in bed at the same time.

On Sept. 20th, my son, Charles M., was married to Mary Ann McMasters, in Salt Lake City, by Daniel H. Wells.

Attended semi-annual Conference on Oct. 5, at Salt Lake City, being accompanied by Brother David P. Kimball, his son Thomas, and my sister-in-law Fannie Williams. The two latter were married on the 15th.

My first counselor, David P. Kimball, died at St. David on Nov. 21.

In December Apostles Heber J. Grant and Brigham Young, with Sister Young, made us a visit. On the 10th the Apostles, Sister Young, my wife, myself and a few others left St. David, went through Sulphur Springs Valley and along the Gila River, holding meetings at all the settlements. We found, about a mile or two south of Safford, the families of John and Adam Welker camped in wagons on the land where they intended to settle. The Apostles agreed with me that my praise of the Gila Valley had not been extravagant.

In March, 1884, I drove over to the Gila River, and on the 2nd organized the Saints who had settled near Safford. They wishing to perpetuate my name, called themselves the Layton branch; John Welker was appointed presiding Elder.

Attended annual Conference at Salt Lake City in April and brought back a car loaded with Jersey cows, alfalfa seed and potatoes.

In May I bought a grist mill for $10,000, on the Gila River (where Safford now stands) with Jonathan Hoopes as partner. I afterwards bought it all and 160 acres of land also.

On May 17 the Temple at Logan, Utah, was dedicated by President Taylor, which ceremony I did not have the privilege of attending, but my wife Caroline C. was there at the special request of Prest. Taylor.

On May 29 we were called upon to sympathize with our dear friend Wilmuth East, whose husband, Edward Wallace East, a

prominent Elder and faithful worker in the
Church, died at Pima.

The Saints in Utah were now being persecuted under the Edmunds law, but as yet we
had not been troubled here.

On July 5 the Primary Association of St.
Joseph stake was organized with Josephine
Rogers as president; Eliza A. Allred, first,
and Caroline Johnson, second counselors.

Some time in July I bought about 500 head
of Sonora cattle and put them on the ranch
in charge of my son Richard and Joseph Allred. In August I wrote to my wife Rosa H.
to come to Arizona, and I went over to
Safford to get things ready for her, but upon
receiving word from her that she did not
wish to leave Utah, I moved my wife Lizzie
over to Safford mill house, for I was running
the mill and clearing mesquit off the land
which I had bought.

On Sept. 5 my daughter Annie B. was
married to Seth Jones in the Logan Temple in
Utah; she and her husband came to St. David
and taught school there.

One day I received word from the stage

driver that my wives Rosa H. and Septima S. were at Bowie, so I took a team and went over there. Found that they had written to me when they had concluded to come but I, not having received it, had not been at Bowie when they arrived, which was a great disappointment to them. We came back to Safford on Sept. 15, and after staying there for two or three weeks I settled my wife Septima S. and family at Curtis, while the boys took my wife Rosa Ann over to St. David. Her son Isaac was very sick, but she gave him such good and careful nursing that he recovered.

In November my wife Rosa Ann came to Safford and my wife Lizzie went back to St. David.

Nov. 4, the Layton branch was organized as a ward, John Welker, Bishop.

On Dec. 27 a little son was born to my wife Septima S. at Curtis, whom we called Jesse Monroe.

On Dec. 7 I visited the territorial prison at Yuma with Apostle Francis M. Lyman to see Brothers Tenney and Christopherson, who were incarcerated there for conscience' sake.

On Jan. 8, 1885, Alex. F. McDonald, John Campbell and I started on a trip through Mexico to see about renting or buying land on which to locate families of Saints who were being driven into exile because of the Edmunds law. The federal courts and officers were carrying their persecutions to such an extent that many of the brethren were imprisoned and their families scattered. After going through Chihuahua, and the valleys lying on the eastern slope of the Sierra Madres we arrived at Corralitos and found some families ready for settlement in the new country. Among others here who were looking over the country for colonizing purposes was a lord of noble lineage from England, and we enjoyed talking with him of old home scenes.

On arriving at St. David I found that while I was away, President John Taylor, Apostles Joseph F. Smith, Erastus Snow, and Moses Thatcher, also George Reynolds, John Q. Cannon, and others, had come to our house and had then gone on to Guaymas, Mexico, from which trip they returned the day after I arrived. A few days later I went to Salt Lake

City with them. While in Mexico I obtained silk handkerchiefs and neckties for each of my family, both in Arizona and Utah, which act of thoughtfulness seemed to please all of them very much.

From Salt Lake City I went on to Kaysville and while there received a letter from Arizona telling me that on Feb. 12 a pair of twin girls had come to my wife Lizzie W. at St. David. We named them Lillian and Luella.

In March we held our quarterly Conference and for the next few months my time was fully occupied with stake duties; as the stake extended over 100 miles I was riding around a great deal, in order to keep in contact with all the branches of the work.

In June my wife Rosa H. and family went back to Utah, leaving her son, Albert T., with us. I moved my wife Lizzie and family over to the mill at Safford.

We held our June Conference at Pima.

About the first of September a feeling of anxiety and uneasiness depressed my spirit and I told my friends that I knew some of my family in Utah must be in trouble of some kind, and after a few days I received a telegram from my wife Sarah, telling me of the death of our son, Hyrum, which had occurred on the 17th of September. In a few days a letter came in which we were told how Hyrum had been afflicted with rheumatism of a very severe nature for about a month. It must have been a very hard task to have handled him while he was helpless for he was a large man, weighing about 340 pounds.

At our quarterly Conference we had the pleasure of entertaining Apostles Erastus Snow and Brigham Young and received instructions from them.

In October, Wm. D. Johnson was set apart as my first counselor in the stake presidency.

In November I moved my wife Septima S. and family over to St. David.

On Nov. 30 we had a large meeting at my house at Safford and while we were enjoying the spirit of brotherly love and union, some Indians came to the window (as we found out by the moccasin tracks) and seeing so many people together, they knew the settlements must

be almost deserted, so they went on to Layton
ward, stole a number of horses and took them
away with them. They were followed by a
posse of citizens and when crowded quite close
they turned the horses loose. These were re-
captured but the Indians shot among the men
and two brothers—Lorenzo and Seth Wright
—were killed.

I was holding meeting at Pima the next
day, Dec. 1, but I felt very uneasy and rest-
less, and thinking something must be wrong
at home, I excused myself and left the meeting. I rode along very much depressed in
spirit, for several miles, when I saw some
men coming rapidly toward me. I felt intu-
itively that they were the ones who would tell
me bad news. When they met me they
stopped and told me the fearful tale of the
death of these faithful brothers. The sympathy of our people was very sincere for the
widows and little children thus bereft of their
protectors.

During this month many of the Saints who
had been camping on Casas Grande River in
Chihuahua, Mex., moved to the Peadres

Verdes River, which townsite they named Juarez.

On Jan. 1, 1886, my daughter Amy C. was married to Reuben W. Fuller at St. David by Bishop Peter Loughgreen.

On Feb. 8 my son Richard G. led to the altar one of Zion's fair daughters—Annie E. Horne—and they were married at St. David by the Bishop of that place—Peter Loughgreen.

On March 21 Seymour B. Young being with us, we organized the Eighty-ninth quorum of Seventies at Pima.

In the last of March my wife Septima, with five children, left for Utah, going with others who went by teams; her son Oscar driving her wagon. It was a hard trip, but after about six weeks they safely arrived at their destination.

In May we turned all hands who could work on the canal and we brought it down through the valley, I doing about half the work and therefore owning half of the canal.

I received a letter from Utah telling of the

marriage of my son James Albert to Edith
Harrod on May 27, at Kaysville, by Bishop
Peter Barton.

The Saints were wanting to settle close together, so I bought a 600-acre tract of land
of a syndicate living in Tucson, then I bought
out the squatters' right and improvements by
taking quit-claim deeds of them. Thus I was
in a position to help the Saints to get homes.
In July I bought 320 acres of Peter Anderson
(adjoining the other tract) and laid it out in
a townsite which we named Thatcher. I built
a three-roomed adobe house in Thatcher ward
(it being the second house built on the townsite), and we moved into it. I also built a
barn. I gave a lot for a schoolhouse and the
few Saints who were settling here then built
an adobe building on it. The mesquit was so
thick that when we tried to go any place we
were very fortunate if we did not get lost. I
gave the Seventies a lot, but they never made
any use of it; also gave the Bishop a lot for
tithing purposes. The Academy was afterwards built upon it.

On Sept. 2 our house at Safford was filled

with a joyous company, for on that day my son Joseph was married to Cynthia Fife.

The persecutions under the Edmunds law were continuing and many families were in exile, some going to Mexico, while many of the Saints came here and I was kept busy helping them to settle on the townsite, and aiding them to get a start in a new country. Nearly all the leading men of our Church were in hiding, paying fines or in prison; my son-in-law, Wm. Galbraith, having his share of imprisonment with the rest. The United, States deputies were raiding all the settlements throughout Utah and even in Arizona, so that it was indeed an anxious time.

President John Taylor sent a company of explorers into British Columbia and Alberta, Canada, to select a tract of land for a colony. They chose a place in Alberta and named Cardston in honor of their leader, Charles O. Card. Four of my sons afterward settled there.

On Jan. 13, 1887, a bill repealing the anti-Mormon test oath in Arizona was passed by the council branch of the Arizona Legislature.

The house passed it the following day and the governor signed it on Jan. 15.

On Feb. 15 the Edmunds-Tucker bill was adopted by the United States House and Senate and the act became a law without the signature of the President. Under the provisions of this law a United States receiver took possession of Church offices and a wholesale confiscation of Church property was threatened.

April 7 will be remembered as a joyous day, for then my two sons Heber C. and Albert T. were married at Layton, Heber having chosen Agnes Almeda Welker as his bride, while Albert selected Almeda Tibbetts. I performed the ceremony.

Utah was again arranging to demand Statehood. The State convention met, and after several days adopted a constitution on July 5 —one feature of which was the anti-polygamy clause. .President John Taylor was still in exile and was very sick at Kaysville. On July 18, Presidents Geo. Q. Cannon, Joseph F. Smith and others went to him and watched at his bedside; and on the 25th he died at the

15

house of Thos. F. Rouche. The funeral was held in Salt Lake City on the 29th, after which a council meeting decided that the counselors should preside until the Twelve could get together. On Aug. 3, at another council meeting, Brothers Cannon and Smith were reinstated in their places in the Twelve, and the Twelve were sustained as the Presidency of the Church. On Aug. 20 the remains of President John Taylor were transferred to a granite sepulchre in Salt Lake City cemetery.

In the fall of this year I built a small store building of brick, thinking there were now enough settlers here to justify the transaction; I put in a small amount of goods.

On Nov. 11 a little daughter was born to my wife Lizzie, at Thatcher, and we named her Priscilla.

In December we received word from Utah that the "poetess of Israel," Eliza R. Snow, who was president of all Relief Societies in the Church, had died in Salt Lake City on the 5th.

Awaking very early one morning in December with a feeling that something was wrong, I arose and built a fire in the fire-

place and also in the stove. About 5 a. m.
Joseph Allred came in with Apostle Brigham
Young, having come over from St. David in
the night. They were thankful for the warm
fire which greeted them, and also that I obeyed
the impression which I had that some one
needed a good fire; they stayed with us several days.

On Feb. 13, 1888, my daughter Eliza A.,
her husband, Joseph Allred, and their family
moved over to Thatcher from St. David; they
lived with my daughter Amy, while they built
a house for themselves.

We were trying to improve our town a little
and I had shade trees set out for a mile along
Main street and the sidewalk cleared and lev-
eled, which added much to the beauty as well
as the convenience of walking.

On May 19 my daughter Selina C., her husband, Edward Phillips, and their family of
five children arrived from Utah. They were
accompanied by my son Chauncey W. and had
been five weeks on the journey with teams.
They brought their furniture and provisions
with them; also scrapers and farm implements.

They lived with my son Joseph for a few weeks while they built a brick house.

At the annual Conference in Salt Lake City, on April 7, 1889, a First Presidency was sustained, consisting of Wilford Woodruff as President and Geo. Q. Cannon and Joseph F. Smith, counselors; this being the fourth time that a First Presidency had been established in the Church.

In June I took a contract to carry United States mail from Bowie to Ft. Thomas; also from Ft. Thomas to Globe; also Ft. Thomas to Ft. Grant, and Bowie to Ft. Bowie.

In the fall I remodeled the mill at Safford, enlarging its capacity.

In September the Saints living north of Kaysville were organized into a ward and they named it East Layton in honor of our family.

In November the Endowment House—which had been erected in 1855—and in which so many of my children, wives and myself had been sealed and had had the privilege of its sacred ordinances, was torn down.

On Jan. 5, 1890, a little daughter came to my wife Lizzie W. and we named her Minnie.

During this year nearly all the civil rights left to the Saints in Utah were threatened by proposed anti-Mormon legislation (the Liberals being in power).

In July the United States contract took effect, and I also secured the contract from the United States to supply San Carlos Indian reservation with 10,000 pounds of flour a week. As this had to be freighted, the work used about eighty horses, and my sons and sons-in-law were kept busy at work; they always worked together very harmoniously. I built a house at Bowie, also a stable for the horses which were used a sa relay for the stage; some of my sons or sons-in-law taking charge of the business there; I (or one of my sons) going there once a month to pay off the men.

On Sept. 24, President Woodruff issued a manifesto "advising the Saints to refrain from contracting any marriage forbidden by the law of the land." This became a subject for general discussion and at the semi-annual Conference on Oct. 4, 5 and 6, in Salt Lake City, it was accepted by unanimous vote.

In April, 1891, I sold my store to my son

Joseph (but I bought it back in about a year). My time was fully occupied as I had many business interests besides my Church duties; the town of Thatcher was growing in population, land was being cleared, shade trees planted, and grain being put in; also many fields were sowed in alfalfa. The other wards were also settling rapidly and I visited all of them twice each year. The Lord blessed me with good health and strength and my faith in the Priesthood and the Gospel was strong.

On March 17, 1892, the fiftieth anniversary of the Relief Society was celebrated throughout the Church. We had a very enjoyable time in this stake.

Attended the Conference in April at Salt Lake City. President Lorenzo Snow on the 6th explained the order of ceremony at the laying of the capstone of the Temple and trained the congregation in shouting "Hosannah," after which remarks were made by President Wilford Woodruff. The congregation then proceeded to the Temple in procession, when the capstone of the Temple was laid amid great enthusiasm and rejoicing,

President Woodruff pressing the electric button which caused the stone to be lowered to its place. After the shouting of "Hosannah," the vast congregation, on motion of Apostle Francis M. Lyman, voted that the Temple should be finishcd by April 6, 1893. About 40,000 people were present and participated in the ceremonies.

On the evening of the 7th the statue of Moroni on the main east tower and the spire on the middle west tower of the Temple were beautifully illuminated with incandescent lights for the first time.

On April 11 a little son came to my wife Lizzie W. at Thatcher, and we named him Gilbert.

Our family had another joyous occasion on May 24, when my son Oscar and Lula Lewis were married at Thatcher, my counselor Wm. D. Johnson performing the ceremony.

On Oct. 12 the First Presidency of the Church issued a certificate to me as an Elder to preach the Gospel in the United States and to administer in all the ordinances pertaining to that office.

In the spring of 1893 I sold the Safford mill to J. T. Owens.

Went up to Utah in April to Conference and the dedication of the Temple at Salt Lake City. The services were repeated almost daily from the 6th to the 24th. Thirty-one meetings were held, which were attended by a total of nearly 75,000 people.

On the 23rd the Temple was opened for ordinance work under the immediate direction of the First Presidency.

About 7,000 people from Utah visited the World's Fair in Chicago.

During the year 1894 President Cleveland pardoned all polygamists and restored them to their rights.

In January I received news from Utah of the death (on the 16th) of my old friend and associate, Wm. R. Smith, whose counselor I had been for many years in the Davis stake.

On May 19 a little daughter came to my wife Lizzie W., whom we named Elizabeth.

In June I sold the store to my son-in-law, Joseph G. Allred.

On the last day of August (31st) my son

Frederick was married to Barbara Allen Mc-
Guire at Thatcher, Brother Wm. D. Johnson
performing the ceremony.

This valley was now dotted over with
homes of the settlers and we had quite large
assemblages at our quarterly conferences. Our
schools were being well attended; each ward
had one or more schoolhouses. The Lord's
blessing rested upon us and we prospered; our
hearts were united in the cause of Truth. The
engineers had been through our valley and
staked out a line for a railroad; the grading
of the road gave employment to some of our
newcomers.

In October I attended Conference in Salt
Lake City, and while in Kaysville I bought
materials for running an ice factory and
creamery.

In January, 1895, the railroad, named the
Gila Valley, Globe and Northern, was completed as far as Pima and we enjoyed seeing
the cars traversing our beautiful valley.

In the spring I put the ice plant into operation in a building which I had built at Thatcher. This was the worst enterprise I ever un-

dertook and I became almost discouraged
several times, for I had put so much money
into it and for more than a year we could get
nothing but *frost* on the pipes. I sent around
to Globe and other places and finally found another engine. In July I had a well dug back
of the factory, the engine pumping water and
also running the ice plant. We supplied the
valley with ice all that summer, and it was a
blessing to many of us in the hot sultry days.

From news received from Utah I learned
that my son David E. was chosen Bishop of
the West Layton ward, when it was organized on Feb. 22.

CHAPTER XIV.

APPROACHING THE END.

Honorably Released as Stake President—Rapidly
Failing Health—Choice Reunions and Blessings—Prepares to Go Home to Utah.

AFTER all the trials which Utah had made
for Statehood, she was at last rewarded,
for on January 4, 1896, President Grover
Cleveland signed the proclamation which ad-
mitted her into the sisterhood of States.

I attended annual Conference at Salt Lake
City at which time Moses Thatcher was not
upheld as one of the Twelve, because of his
refusal to sign a manifesto issued by the general authorities of the Church to the Saints, in
which the leading men of the Church were requested to seek counsel before accepting political offices which would interfere with their
ecclesiastical duties. His certificate to preach

the Gospel was also revoked. I felt very sad over this occurrence, for Brother Thatcher was a great friend of mine.

Our community was called upon to mourn the death of my second counselor, Brother Morgan Henry Merrill, who left us on July 26th. He was a good, faithful Saint and his loss was felt in the entire stake.

On Sept. 4 another little daughter was added to our household, coming to my wife Lizzie W. and we named her Wilmuth.

On Nov. 13 my business called me to the lower end of the valley, and as I was not feeling very well, I asked my son-in-law, E. C. Phillips, to accompany me. I hoped the ride in the fresh air would benefit me, but I was disappointed for I did not feel any better. I finished my business at Geronimo and we started on the return trip, but I continued to feel worse; when between Thomas and Pima I was attacked with severe cramps, which continued all night and for several days without much relief.

In December my sons Charles and Samuel came from Utah to visit me and stayed two or three weeks with us, but I still remained confined to my bed.

I traded property in February, 1897, with my son Joseph, and moved into his house. I was enough better that I could walk around out of doors some each day. I remodeled the house somewhat.

My son Charles M. and his family arrived from Utah on March 17, and moved into my old house.

In May I was again confined to my bed, and on the 10th I felt very uneasy and as if something was wrong with my son Joseph, who had been under the doctor's care at Safford for several days. Although I asked questions about him, the answers were evasive, but the next morning they told me he was dead. The funeral services were held at Thatcher, Brothers Wm. Packer and Benjamin Peel being the chief speakers. He was interred in the Thatcher cemetery.

My health did not become better although sometimes I felt a little better for a few days, then some days I had excruciating pains; but the Lord gave me patience and endurance to bear my sufferings.

In January, 1898, I received the following letter from the First Presidency at Salt Lake City:

Salt Lake City, Utah,
January 21st, 1898.
President Christopher Layton,
St. Joseph Stake.

DEAR BROTHER LAYTON—A short time ago a member of your family had a conversation with Elder Brigham Young in relation to your physical condition, in which it was represented that your health was such as to render it almost impossible for you to give that attention to the interests of' the Stake which it requires, and that it would be a great relief for you to be released from the duties now devolving upon you as its president.

This information which Brother Young had received from a member of your family, he reported to a late meeting of the First Presidency and Apostles, with a recommendation that the suggested change be made and that a younger and more active man be appointed to succeed you. We may say, that we ourselves and the members of the Council generally have

understood that your health for some time
past has been in quite a poor state, and that it
has been with difficulty that you have been
able to attend to your stake duties.   After
fully considering this matter, the Council unanimously decided to honorably release you as
President of the St. Joseph stake, and to appoint Andrew Kimball, a son of the late President Heber C. Kimball, to be your successor,
your release to take· effect when he shall be
installed.

We trust this action will receive your un-
qualified approval, and that you will receive
it in the spirit in which it is made, and give to
Brother Kimball your sympathy and hearty
support, and help him in every way you possibly can to establish himself and family in
your midst, and in the hearts of the people, for
we feel that, although the state of your health
has incapacitated you for the more active work
such as is required in a stake like St. Joseph,
which covers so much country, you can, nevertheless, be of great use and benefit, and your
influence may also be exerted for great good,
in assisting and supporting Brother Kimball in
the labors and duties which shall be required
of him.

We feel that the Lord will accept of your
labors in the St. Joseph stake, and that he
will bless and reward you for your long years

of faithful service in the Church, and continue
to bless you as our fellow servant.

With kindest regards, we are
Your brethren,
WILFORD WOODRUFF,
GEO. Q. CANNON,
JOS. F. SMITH.

P. S.—Elders John Henry Smith and John
W. Taylor have been appointed to attend your
Conference on the 30th and 31st inst. for the
purpose of installing Brother Kimball as your
successor; and they have been authorized to
reorganize the High Council and such part of
the stake as they may deem necessary, and we
trust that yourself and the officers and Saints
generally will give these brethren your fullest
and heartiest support in whatever changes they
may see proper to make.

W. W.
G. Q. C.
J. F. S.

On Jan. 27, Apostles John Henry Smith
and John W. Taylor came from Utah to attend to the business of St. Joseph stake. The
wards and stake were disorganized, every one
receiving an honorable release from their labors, on the 28th, then on the 29th the stake

was reorganized with Andrew Kimball as president and Wm. D. Johnson as first and Charles M. Layton as second counselors. On the 30th the wards were all reorganized, and on the 31st the High Council was reinstated.

On Sunday, January 30, Brother John Henry Smith spoke to the conference and paid me the following tribute of respect:

President Layton has been an honest and industrious man; his time and means have been at the disposal of the authorities of the Church for the upholding of the Lord's kingdom. In rearing his large family he has done nobly by them, always keeping them employed, and they were a credit to him. He has opened the way by which many families have secured homes and the comforts of life; he has been, and is, a blessing to thousands; he has his faults and has made mistakes, but not serious ones. I regard him as a generous, high-minded gentleman, one who has made the world much better by having lived in it. He gave his young manhood to preserve the liberty of the people he loved so well; his mature judgment and great common sense have been freely utilized for the extension of Zion; in his declining days and as he is hastening to

16

the Great Beyond to make his reckoning there,
I say of him, he is one of God's jewels, and
that his name is written in the Lamb's book
of life. I bless him and his posterity forever.

BLESSING

*Given by Philemon C. Merrill, patriarch, at
Thatcher, Arizona, April 20, 1898.*

Brother Christopher Layton, I place my
hands upon your head—having been set apart
and ordained as a patriarch—and in the authority thereof I bless you and pray that God will
dictate by the spirit that which I shall say, for
by that power all blessings come. You are
holding the position that Abraham, Isaac and
Jacob held to bless their children; therefore
thy mind shall be exercised in behalf of thy
posterity, notwithstanding thou mayest be
called to enter a higher sphere of action in
the due time of the Lord; thou shalt exercise in
that sphere a greater influence and power than
thou canst tabernacled as thou art now, for
the spirit cannot expand when it is trammeled
with flesh and blood. Brother Layton, thou
shalt always have in thy posterity a representative in the earth, for when thy name is called
there will always be one to answer to that
call; thy work shall proceed onward until the

end of the earth, and as one of the patriarchs
thou wilt administer blessings upon thy children's children and that spirit which has ac-
tuated the patriarchs of old shall be carried
on in the lineage of which thou art, even that
of Levi, for in that tribe they will offer an of-
ering in righteousness in the earth in the flesh,
for thou hast already obtained the same blessings that were sealed upon Abraham, Isaac
and Jacob. Thou hast received in the house
of God all thine anointings, all that was or
ever will be given to man in the flesh. All
thy faults have gone before thee, and are can-
celled in the earth and in the heavens. They
children will bless thee and remember thee in
fond remembrance and carry on the great work
which shall complete thine exaltation, for thou
shalt stand on the right hand of Joseph and
Hyrum in connection with all the prophets
(for thou art an evangelist), clothed upon
with eternal lives. In the resurrection none
will have a more glorified body; therefore I
say unto you, be thou blessed with the spirit of
your exaltation, for thou art fully ripe and
prepared to enter into thy rest. Now I seal
these blessings upon you, ratifying your former
blessings that have been placed upon your
head; therefore, be comforted in these sayings
for they are true and faithful, and will be fully
realized by you, when you gaze upon the labors

of your past life in your numerous posterity which shall continue to be upon you and yours throughout the endless ages of eternity. I seal these blessings upon you as a patriarch, in the name of Jesus Christ. Amen.

PATRIARCHAL BLESSING

Given by Samuel Claridge, upon the head of Christopher Layton, at Thatcher, Graham County, Arizona.

Brother Christopher Layton, in the name of the Lord Jesus Christ, I lay my hands upon your head and bestow upon you a father's blessing, which shall be given according to the patriarchal order, that was given to our father Abraham; and Brother Christopher Layton, by virtue of the authority and power that is given me to bless, I bless you and you shall be blessed. God, our heavenly Father, has accepted of your labors and there is a greater reward awaiting you and the glory and power thereof is greater than I can describe. You have been preserved from your infancy from dangers and death in order that you may accomplish a great work upon this earth. The angels of God have shielded you and watched over you in times of danger, and your life has been preserved up to this present time for a wise purpose in your heavenly Father, and this seeming affliction that you have passed through, and are still passing through, shall be sanctified to your good and redound to your glory, and you shall yet say, "How kind and merciful my Father in heaven has dealt with me." It will not be long before your spirit will pass by on the other side, and there you will meet your wives and children, your father and mother, the Prophets and Apostles who have died, and they will honor you and respect you and you shall have a glorious time, and these light afflictions shall be but a bubble compared to the glory and happiness that await you there. You are a child of Abraham, through the loins of Joseph, and all the blessings that were promised upon him that was sold into Egypt shall be yours: your children shall be great and mighty in the priesthood and none shall excel them in all Israel: they shall become a power in Israel for the building up of Zion. You shall see Zion redeemed, you shall come in the clouds of heaven with Christ, our Redeemer, and all his holy angels. You shall enter into that glorious temple that shall be reared in Jackson county, and there you shall meet your children's children, who will be upon the earth and your ancestors that have lived for generations past shall reap the benefit of your visits to that holy temple.

I now say, God bless you and may the angels of peace watch over you and bear you up in their arms, that peace may be upon you from this time, henceforth and forever. All these blessings I seal upon you and you shall realize the fulfillment of them all, which I promise in the name of Jesus. Amen.

On the morning of Jan. 29, 1898, before going to conference Apostles John Henry Smith and John W. Taylor, accompanied by Andrew Kimball, called at our house. My wife Lizzie was present, and we sent for my sons Charles M. and Richard; also my daughters Eliza and Selina. They all knelt around my bed, John Henry Smith leading in prayer. Then he blessed me, which filled my soul with peace and joy; after which he ordained me a Patriarch, and I bestowed the mantle of my office upon the shoulders of Andrew Kimball.

In the spring my oldest daughter, Elizabeth Galbraith, having heard of my sickness, came from Mexico and stayed with us for about a month. In some respects it was a sorrowful

visit, for her husband had recently passed to
the "other side of the vail," and we both felt
that it was our last visit together on this earth.
While she was here my youngest child, Wilmuth, and she had their picture taken together.
Libby was fifty-four years old, while Wilmuth
was only two years.

On my seventy-seventh birthday, March 8,
although not able to arise, I had the pleasure
of welcoming to our house all of my children
who live in Arizona, their wives and husbands,
President Andrew Kimball, Patriarch P. C.
Merrill and wife, Brother E. M. Curtis and
wife, and Dr. Karl G. Maeser. We sang, "We
thank Thee, O God, for a prophet;" then my
son-in-law Joseph G. Allred offered a prayer,
followed by some remarks by President Kimball; who seemed to be moved by the Spirit as
he talked to us of the necessity of having a
family organization, and said he would like
to see one in this family, which idea was well
received by all present. Then Charles talked
to us, followed by Brother Merrill, his wife,
Cyrena, my wife Lizzie, my daughters Selina
and Eliza, all of which was very consoling,

and we all felt the good influence of the Spirit of the Lord with us. President Kimball suggested that a committee of the family be appointed to look up my genealogy and write a history of my life.

We elected my daughter Selina Phillips as the secretary for this work, with Charles and Richard to assist her. Sister Sylvia L. Sessions was chosen and engaged for the scribe. We also chose a committee to assist us in this work who live in Kaysville, Utah, namely: Christopher Layton, Jun., Mary Ann Swan and Annie B. Jones. Patriarch Merrill also offered to assist us in every way that he could.

I then gave my children a family blessing and admonished them to remain true to the Gospel of Christ; never to consider their calling a task, but to regard it as a pleasure; to always honor whatever office they were called upon to fill and to never obligate themselves farther than they could see their way clear. Brother Kimball said he should be pleased to consider himself a member of this family and would take pleasure in doing anything in his power to assist us in this work. After singing, Brother Merrill pronounced a benediction.

As I was now much wearied, the company all departed and with a prayer in my heart for them and my other families in Utah I composed myself to rest. I often wondered why it was that I must suffer so long and intensely, but Dr. Maeser said "it was that I might learn the lesson of patience." I think he was right.

In May my wife Caroline came from Utah to visit us and stayed about six weeks.

In June I made up my mind to pass my last days with my family and friends in Utah, and consult physicians in Salt Lake City about the advisability of undergoing an operation for my complaint.

I will leave here in a few days. One thought which is a great comfort to me is that not one of my children ever apostatized. I now ask God's blessings upon all who shall read this history of my life; may they be faithful to do the will and work of our heavenly Father; that they may have peace, joy and happiness, an increase of wisdom, knowledge and the power of God; outside of this there are no promised blessings. May they help each other to be better and happier; cultivate and preserve an enlightened conscience and follow the Holy Spirit; hold fast to what is good, endure to the end and great shall be your reward for your trials and heart-yearnings and tears; yea, our God will give you a crown of unfading glory through the countless ages of eternities.

[With the above impressive prayer and testimony closes the autobiography of Christopher Layton—that is, the personal sketch of his life as dictated by, or read to and approved by him. The brief story of his final return to his old home at Kaysville, and his death, together with the full proceedings of his funeral, and the loving tribute headed "Personal Characteristics," which constitute the following chapter, was prepared by the committees representing the family, referred to on page 234 and in the Introduction to this little volume.

J. Q. C.]

CHAPTER XV.

The Last Journey—Undergoes operation—Death on
Aug. 7, 1898—Impressive Funeral—Personal
characteristics.

ON June 13, 1898, our father, Christopher
Layton, left for Utah. He had been sick
for over a year and a half, and at many times
we had thought he could not live longer, but in
answer to prayers and administrations by the
Priesthood, his wonderful vitality again as-
serted itself.

Several days before his departure, we had
telegraphed for a through parlor car, and received reply that the railroad company would
take him to Kaysville, Utah, without change of
cars or delay. His wife Lizzie, and our brothers Charles and Richard accompanied him to
Bowie, where the parlor car was to meet him.

He bore the trip with fortitude but grew
slightly impatient while waiting at Bowie, for

he feared his strength would fail before he could reach his journey's end. When every arrangement for his comfort was completed and the train left for California, Richard sadly returned to Thatcher, feeling that he had parted from our father for the last time on earth.

The trip was very comfortable, and he rested as easily as if at home. On arriving at Oakland, Cal., they were informed that they must change cars. Father walked the length of the long train and into the depot, where they were obliged to remain a half hour, then walk again quite a distance to the other car; and when they were again on the train, he was completely exhausted and for a while it seemed as if he could not possibly survive to reach his destination; but at last his system responded to the restoratives used and again he rested comfortably. He had no appetite for anything, nothing seemed to tempt him to eat, until from the dining car were procured some fresh green peas, which he really enjoyed.

On arriving at Ogden, Utah, he was met by his sons and daughters and Apostle Richards, who took charge of him, while they again

changed cars. He now appeared to be much
better and was able to converse pleasantly all
the rest of the trip.

They arrived in Kaysville on Friday, June
17, and many relatives and friends called to
welcome him back home.

As soon as he was somewhat rested from the
journey he began to suffer severe pain at intervals until, about the first of July, it was
deemed best to have a surgical operation performed. Drs. Richards and Wilcox were the
operating physicians and father bore the ordeal
well, though from having taken so much mor-
phine and chloroform, he was unconscious
from 5 o'clock in the afternoon until the next
morning at 2 o'clock, when he rallied and improved beyond the expectations of his doctors
and friends. He was never able to move around
the house, although, at times, in fatherly so-
licitude, he gave kind counsel and admonitions
to his wives, children and friends.

Rather unexpectedly, on Sunday, August 7,
he appeared to be failing. Members of the
family were immediately notified and, surrounded by his families, honored and beloved

by them all, he peacefully fell asleep and his spirit was with God.

The relatives from Arizona arrived at Kaysville on Friday and the funeral was held in the meeting house on Saturday, Aug. 13, at 2 o'clock p. m.

The bishop of the ward, Peter Barton, showed him honor by purchasing beautiful mourning decorations for the house, which was filled with a sympathizing assemblage.

The proceedings at the funeral services here follow in full:

FUNERAL.

"Hark! from afar the funeral knell
Moves on the breeze, its echoes swell!"

PRAYER BY STAKE PRESIDENT JOHN W. HESS.

Our Father who art in heaven, we have met here together today on this solemn occasion to pay unto one of thy faithful servants our respect and the gratitude that we feel towards Thee, our Father. We realize, our Heavenly Father, that it is in Thy providence that we should come into this world and take upon us a

body, and to lay a foundation for our future
existence; and that it is also in thy providence
that we should lay down these tabernacles that
we have taken upon us when the time comes,
until the time of the resurrection. These are
fixed providences which we fully understand.
And Father, inasmuch as we have come together here today to show our respect and
our honor to this thy servant that has been
called away from us, we have come, Father,
feeling that it is also in thy providence that
we have the privilege of doing so under these
favorable circumstances; because we do know
that thy people have fallen by the way; they
have been left upon the plain; they have been
left under various circumstances which were
not as favorable as those which confront us
this day. We thank thee, O our God, that thou
hast been thus mindful of us, that thou hast in
thy providence watched over us, and that thy
care has been over us, that we have been preserved, and that many of us still live and still
have a fixed desire in our hearts to serve thee,
and to fill up our days in helping to build up
thy kingdom, as this thy servant President
Layton has done. O God, our Father, we feel
in our hearts that thy servant has been one of
thy chosen servants, and that he has performed
a great and mighty work, and that he has been
faithful even unto the end; and that he has

laid down his tabernacle with his spirit filled
with the testimony of the Lord Jesus. Father,
we thank thee for this blessing, that this thy
servant has thus been faithful, and pray that we
may be enabled to emulate his example in our
lives, and labor faithfully as he has done; and
when our time shall come, that it may be said
that we have been faithful to the last. Father,
we do not feel that there is any occasion here
today to mourn, or to feel a regret that thy
providence has removed from us this thy servant; but Father, we feel to thank thee, we
feel to thank and to bless thy holy name, that
thy servant has thus been faithful, and that
he has laid a foundation that will never be
thrown down. Father, wilt thou bless his posterity, his numerous posterity of sons and
daughters and wives; may their hearts be comforted this day, our Father, and may they, instead of mourning, feel to rejoice in their
hearts that they are representing so noble a
character, so faithful a husband and father;
that they may rejoice in thy goodness to him,
for the care and protection that has been over
him, that he has lived to a good age; and that
they may emulate all his good examples, and
that they also at the proper time may rejoice
in heaven, faithful to the end. Father, bless us
here this day; may the solemnity of this occasion rest upon each one of us, and may our

hearts be open to the words of truth that we may hear from thy servants. Father, we also thank thee for the privilege of having with us one of the Presidents of thy Church, even Pres-ident Smith and Apostle Smith also, and Pres-ident Seymour B. Young; that we are so high-ly favored, that we are honored with their presence. And we pray that thou wilt bless them, and inspire them with the feeling that they may talk those things to us that shall be for our good; that we may be strengthened and have power to go forth and do good in the earth. We dedicate ourselves, together with the labors and services of this afternoon, and all that pertains unto us, and pray that thy care and protection and peace may be over us continually; which we ask in the name of Jesus Christ our Redeemer. Amen.

"Nearer, my God, to Thee, nearer to Thee," by the choir.

REMARKS BY PRESIDENT JOSEPH F. SMITH.

Contrary somewhat to my usual custom, and not altogether in accordance with my nat-ural desire, I rise to speak to you as the Lord may give me utterance, at the beginning of this meeting. I would very much prefer to listen and to keep my seat, than to occupy this posi-

17

tion myself, for I could satisfy my mind and
my spirit better, I think, so far as I am person-
ally concerned, in reflection and in listening to
the thoughts expressed by others, than it will
be possible for me to do in attempting to speak
to you. I do not feel that there should be here
present a spirit of mourning or of lamentation;
and we have not met together under such an
influence or with such a spirit hovering over
us. On the contrary we have met together to
rejoice as well as to mourn; and we feel grateful and thankful to the Lord our God, as well
as to feel, or to sense the feeling of depriva-
tion, of loneliness and of sadness which comes
to us by reason of the departure from us of one
who has been for so many, many years so fa-
miliar to us, and of one upon whom so many
have looked with dependence for guidance and
for counsel and for support.

We have on this occasion before us the remains of a very notable man, a man of strong
individuality, and of great physical and mental
power and magnetism; a man who was fitted
and qualified by nature to be a leader among
men, and a power in the midst of his fellow
creatures. He, Brother Christopher Layton,
was no common man; he was no ordinary in-
dividual; he was a rare man. He was one
among a thousand. Although lacking in education, in the esteem as it is reckoned by the

world, yet mentally and intellectually he was capacitated to cope with the most learned in relation to the management of the material affairs of life; and there were few men really his equal in relation to the management of temporal affairs. He was a vigorous, energetic, clear-minded, conscientious man, and a man whose natural qualifications fitted him for many responsible public duties and positions in the midst of the Saints and in the midst of the people wherever he has dwelt. My recollection goes back to a very early day, when Bishop Layton, as we used to call him familiarly, was the bishop of this ward. In those early days Kaysville was not what it is today. I remember it at that time, or in those days, as almost a barren waste; one of the most forbidding, uninviting regions that could be found in all this vast barren valley; when Bishop Layton was the bishop here. That is in the beginning of his bishopric; although at that time this region of country began to look up and become prosperous. Before that I believe Bishop Allen Taylor was bishop. I have passed through here when it was impossible to find a spear of hay or anything better than wheat chaff or oat straw with which to feed a team. But under the bishopric of our beloved brother whose remains now lie before us, a change came over the face of this land, and it began to be prosperous, and the people began to be prosperous in it; for the Lord blessed the earth here, and by the aid of lucerne, which seemed to be so naturally adapted to the climate here, everything seemed to take a start in the upward direction. After serving for many years as bishop, he was chosen as a counselor in the presidency of this stake of Zion when this stake was organized. And he remained counselor in the presidency of the stake until circumstances arose which made it necessary for his personal safety, not because of any crime or misdemeanor in the eye of God or of any righteous man, but personal safety, made it necessary for him to seek a home in another part of our land. And in the course of time he became the president of the Saint Joseph stake of Zion in Arizona; and remained the president of that stake, prosperously guiding and directing the energies of the people in that region of country until his health failed him and he was stricken with weakness, until it was impossible for him to attend to the duties of his calling. And under these circumstances it was deemed wisdom to release him from the arduous duties as president of the Saint Joseph stake and ordain him a patriarch, and place a younger man in the position of president of that stake of Zion. And soon after this, his health failing, he returned here to Kaysville, to his former home

and to the scenes of his former activity and
to the associations of his former days, to end
his mortal life among his old friends and in the
midst of his family.

Brother Layton had reached an advanced
age, not as old as he might have been, possibly,
if he had been more cautious and careful of
his health, and had not been so inured to hardships and to activity and to toil and labor; for
it is a fact that while a certain amount of energy and of activity is productive of health and
the prolongation of life, yet when the mental
and the physical powers are overtaxed by too
arduous labor and too great a strain, both the
mind and the body must yield to the undue
pressure upon it, and under such circumstances
life is often cut short. I believe that President
Layton, or Patriarch Layton, with his natural
energy and vital force, if he had been more
cautious or careful of his health all through,
might have lived to a very great age. But he
has worn out in the service of the Lord, and
in the service of the people of God, and in the
service of his family. He has not rusted out.
He has not fallen to pieces by disuse or anything of this kind, for he was always energetic;
he was always active; he was always persever-
ing; and he was always pushing and forging
ahead for something that would be of vast importance to mankind; so that nothing too good

can be said of our beloved brother and friend, Bishop Layton. I have but one regret in my heart, and that is that I did not lay aside my duties and my cares and responsibilities that continue to press upon me, during his last illness to come here and see him; make him a visit and renew our association; for I have labored with him in times past. Some of you will remember that in the presidency of Brigham Young, I myself acted as the president of this stake of Zion, although it was not at that time organized into a stake. But I was appointed by President Young to labor here as the presiding officer over Davis county. President Layton was one of my right hand men, one of my active advisers and helpers, and I learned to appreciate his work and his ability as a man almost endowed with real genius in many respects. And I was acquainted with him in the days of his bishopric, and in the days of my presidency here, and also in the days of his associations with President Smith and President Hess here; and I have been acquainted with him ever since his appointment to the presidency of the stake of Zion. And all through I have been pleased and gratified with my acquaintance with so noble and so faithful and so energetic a man.

Now my brothers and sisters, it matters not in relation to these things, about our tempor-

alities. I might spend all the moments that
were allotted to me here in eulogies of Brother
Layton, but it would amount to but little after
all. Some of you knew him more than I did,
and I am thankful for it, and I feel to say God
bless the family of Brother Christopher Layton.
He has done a great work in the earth, and I
tell you that he has made his calling and election about as sure as almost any man I think
that ever lived in the flesh, so far as that is
concerned. I want to read a few words. The
Lord says:

"Behold! mine house is a house of order,
saith the Lord God, and not a house of con-
fusion.

"Will I accept of an offering, saith the Lord,
that is not made in my name?

"Or, will I receive at your hands that which
I have not appointed?

"And will I appoint unto you, saith the
Lord, except it be by law, even as I and my
Father ordained unto you, before the world
was?

"I am the Lord thy God, and I give unto you
this commandment, that no man shall come
unto the Father but by me, or by my word,
which is my law, saith the Lord;

"And everything that is in the world, whether it be ordained by me, by thrones, or prin-

cipalities, or powers, or things of name, whatsoever they may be, that are not by me or by
my word, saith the Lord, shall be thrown
down, and shall not remain after men are dead,
neither in nor after the resurrection, saith the
Lord your God;

"For whatsoever things remain, are by me;
and whatsoever things are not by me, shall be
shaken and destroyed."

Now, there is a principle involved in this,
and it is a principle of vast consequence to the
children of men, and it is a principle that in-
volves the relation that exists today between
him who was Bishop Layton, or President Layton, and this vast concourse of people that I
see before me here, which constitute his wives
and his children and his children's children to
the second or third generation. I want to as-
sure this family and also this vast congregation that those who are associated with Brother Layton have become associated unto him
and with him, by the law of God, and by the
power of the Almighty; and therefore they
will remain in and after the resurrection from
the dead, and there is no power on earth, nor
in the heavens, nor beneath the heavens that
can ever disrupt or destroy the relationships
that have been formed under and in connection with the power of God, and the law of

God, between Brother Layton and his family,
except the power of sin, and that sin on the
part of the individuals themselves. We have
every reason to believe that Brother Layton
himself has been true to his convictions, has
been faithful to the light that he possessed,
and to the intelligence that he possessed, and
the power that he possessed to cope with the
affairs of the world that were arrayed against
him; and that he has been faithful to the last;
and that he has fought the good fight; that he
has kept the faith; that henceforth there is
laid up for him a crown of everlasting life, and
no man can take it from him. Now I want to
say to the family and the children and wives of
Brother Layton, that the relationships that
have been formed between you and this man,
are not relationships that were destined to last
until death should part you and then cease, but
they were relationships that were intended to
exist throughout the countless ages of eternity, because they were by God created,
formed, and entered into and confirmed, and
therefore they are eternal in their nature.

The house of God is a house of order. Let
me read a little more in relation to the covenant of marriage. A distinguishing feature
more than another of his character was that
he was a married man, and he was married by
the law of God.

"Therefore, if a man marry him a wife in the world, and he marry her not by me, nor by my word; and he covenant with her so long as he is in the world, and she with him, their covenant and marriage are not of force when they are dead, and when they are out of the world; therefore, they are not bound by any law when they are out of the world;

"Therefore, when they are out of the world, they neither marry, nor are given in marriage; but are appointed angels in heaven, which angels are ministering servants, to minister for those who are worthy of a far more, and an exceeding, and an eternal weight of glory;

"For these angels did not abide my law, therefore they cannot be enlarged, but remain separately and singly, without exaltation, in their saved condition, to all eternity, and from henceforth are not Gods, but are angels of God, forever and ever."

Then the Lord goes on to say, if a man marry a wife by him and by his law, then that covenant is accepted of the Lord, and it is an eternal covenant, and they go on to increase and continue in life and in death and in the resurrection from the dead, and throughout the countless ages of eternity; and then, says the Lord:

"Then shall they be Gods, because they have

no end; therefore shall they be from everlasting to everlasting, because they continue; then shall they be above all, because all things are subject to them; then shall they be Gods, because they have all power, and the angels are subject unto them.

"Verily, verily I say unto you, except ye abide in my law, ye cannot attain to this glory;

"For strait is the gate, and narrow the way that leadeth unto the exaltation and continuation of the lives, and few there be that find it, because ye receive me not in the world, neither do ye know me.

"But if ye receive me in the world, then shall ye know me, and shall receive your exaltation, that where I am, ye shall be also.

"This is eternal life, to know the only wise and true God, and Jesus Christ, whom he hath sent. I am he. Receive ye, therefore, my law."

I want to say to you that Brother Layton has received this law; Brother Layton has entered into this law. These women that I see before me, that are sealed to him for time and eternity, entered into that covenant by that law, and they are sealed. for time and for all eternity; and they shall not be angels who shall be ministers unto those who are worthy of a far more exceeding and eternal weight of glory; they shall be queens and priestesses unto God, and shall reign in the heavens and in their kingdoms. This is what I wanted to say to this congregation and to his family, and to all who have by the law of God entered into the new and everlasting covenants.

My brethren and sisters, it was a duty that brought me here. I felt that I wanted to come to pay my last tribute of respect to my departed brother. There are others who can speak of his qualifications and of his faithfulness, but my time is short. I came that I might speak a word of comfort to this family; if by any word of mine they could be comforted, made to feel a spirit of happiness and hope, a spirit of forgiveness one towards another, of forgiveness for everything that they have felt was wrong in their lives or in the lives of those with whom they have been associated. If they will forgive one another, and will be worthy of the covenants that they have made, they will reap the reward and they will not be deprived of any blessing that has been promised unto them, nor shall any promise fail that has ever been made to them. His sons shall be blest; his daughters shall be blest; and every child shall be blest in this land that is given unto you. Possess this land and inherit it, and inherit your father's faithfulness to the cause of Zion. Your father has lived and died true to the gospel; and he has lived to set an example of integrity to the cause of Zion. So let me admonish the children of Brother Layton to be true to their covenants and never depart from the right way.

My brethren and sisters, the sons and daughters of Brother Layton, I ask you as a friend and brother, and I ask you in the name of the Lord, as a minister of the gospel of the Lord Jesus Christ, that you will be true to your father, true to your integrity as he has been true to the integrity of the cause of Zion. As he has gone out of the world sure of eternal life and exaltation, so will you each of you in your time follow your father, as sure of exaltation as he is sure of exaltation. Brethren, I would like to spend an hour or so talking with you. I would like to read from the Scriptures the thoughts that are passing through my mind, but my time will not permit. I have another engagement in Salt Lake City a little after four o'clock, and after I shall close my remarks I shall take the liberty of departing from the meeting, leaving the brethren to continue the services. God bless the family, and God bless all that pertains to the children of President Layton; lead them on triumphantly until they shall gain the exaltation that he has gained; where they shall not be angels to minister unto those that are more worthy, but they shall be kings and queens and have everlasting life and eternal increase, which is the gift of God. May the Lord bless you, is my prayer, in the name of Jesus. Amen.

REMARKS BY SEYMOUR B. YOUNG.

President Christopher Layton received many years ago, in the eventful history of his life, a change of heart, and it imprinted itself upon him as a new life, and he became as were the people on the day of Pentecost, a convert to the gospel of the Lord Jesus Christ; and he exclaimed as Ruth exclaimed: "do not persuade me from following after them." He said to the people of the Lord, "whither thou goest I will go, and whither thou diest there I will die also, for thy people shall be my people henceforth;" and this was characteristic of the life of Christopher Layton. I believe that he was a friend of mine, and I am proud to say that I was a very true friend to him so far as I knew how to be. And I say God bless his memory; and I testify that the words spoken by President Joseph F. Smith are true, and they do truly represent the life and character of President Christopher Layton. And I will repeat the words of Whittier, who said: "He has done the work of a true man; crown him, bless him, honor him, and love his name forever." God bless the family of Christopher Layton. God bless you all, my brethren and sisters, and may you seek to exemplify the noble lives that are set before you as leaders, in all your life to come, following the good example of these great men that live and die in our midst. And we have the full testimony that has been read to us today, and that testimony is in every heart, that the Lord has said, seeing the good works of · his faithful servant, "go up higher." May this be the lot of every one of us, to walk faithfully before the Lord, keeping his commandments and magnifying the callings he has placed upon us, doing our whole duty as faithful servants and handmaidens; with the hope that at the end of our days, it may be truthfully said also of us: "he has fought the good fight, he has kept the faith, henceforth there is a crown of glory laid up for him." May this be the well done and happy termination of all of our lives; that we may receive those welcome plaudits, "well done, thou good and faithful servants and handmaidens, enter into the joy of thy Lord." This is the condition I testify today of Christopher Layton. His faithful life has gained this happy result for him. May we also be faithful, is my prayer, in the name of Jesus Christ. Amen.

REMARKS BY APOSTLE JOHN HENRY SMITH.

My brethren and sisters, I am happy in the privilege of attending these services and of adding my tribute of respect to President Layton; as it has fallen to my lot probably more than to any of the associates in my immediate council, to have companionship with President Layton. For the past ten or twelve years, almost yearly, and sometimes twice a year, I have made the tour of the southern stakes of the Church. And through this means have been thrown more or less intimately with President Layton in his field of labor. A year ago last March I was in that part of the country and discovered that he was in a very critical condition physically. Upon my return to Utah, I told the Presidency that it seemed to me that it would be a measure of propriety in the interests of the preservation of his health, that the cares and the labors that were upon him he should be relieved of. They felt, however, that there was no necessity particularly for change under the circumstances, although President Layton had said to me in parting with him, that he felt that he was carrying about all that was possible for him to do, and he would regard it in the light of relief to be freed from his responsibilities. It was my privilege again, during the earlier months of the present year, upon his solicitation and in company with others of the brethren, to make the changes that led to his release from that presidency. And it is always a delicate place to be put in, no matter what the condition of our health or the circumstances surrounding us are, to relieve men who have been strong, determined and capable in the performance of every duty in their lives to the best of their ability. But I believe that his family that were with him in that part of the country will bear us out in this, that in the performance of this duty, we received his blessing and his approval and most kindly feeling in the labor that we had there to perform. And in speaking in the conference where the changes were made, I almost felt in paying a brief tribute to his labors and ministry, that it was like possibly the preaching of his funeral sermon; for it did not seem to me that it was possible that he could last any great length of time; although his great or his splendid constitution seemed to be struggling against the encroachments of disease; and with his heroic courage and determination to bear up to the last minute, no one can tell the possibilities of a man of his type. I desire to endorse with all my heart, the remarks that have been made by my brethren who have preceded me on this occasion. And I think he himself, in possibly the last conversation but one that I ever held with him previous to our separation in Arizona last spring, paid as high a tribute to his own family as any one of us could possibly pay, es-

18

pecially so it is the case in regard to his children. I think several times, however, in my meeting with him, he has made the remark: "I am the father [if I remember the number correctly] of over fifty living children, and I have neither boy or girl that would ever allow me to hitch up or unhitch a horse if they were about the home." I thought in his remark made in regard to this numerous family, it was a tribute probably that few men could pay to their children, even where they had but a limited family of one, two, three, four or five children, and possibly more; and that it spoke volumes for his leadership, the force of his character, and the influence and power that he exercised in the control and government of his family. I have been led to think as I was sitting here upon my seat and listening to the remarks that have been made, what family in this district has been better housed and better fed, that have been kept more industriously at work, than has the family of Brother Layton? Is there any man in the district standing absolutely alone, without wife or child, that has fared better than he has fared, than his family has fared? Or any man with a wife and no children, or with a wife and half a dozen children, that has done his part in a more masterful manner, in providing for the wants and needs, and utilizing the powers and forces that he possessed in directing the improvements and labors of his house, in the accomplishment of their temporal good? And I believe that the same impress of forcefulness manifested in the industry of his household, he has also established and fixed in their spiritual needs. Not that it can be anticipated, nor should be, that there shall not be members of a house of this magnitude that shall not be possessed of faults, that shall not make some mistakes and have some of the weaknesses of human nature. We could not anticipate this. President Layton was possessed of his faults and weaknesses. He made his mistakes. It has fallen to my lot in my companionship with him, to adjust troubles between him and his brethren, and to correct him; and I have noted in connection with this delicate species of labor, that he has never failed so far as he was concerned, to exhibit that degree of humility that was in him; and I have had greater love and respect and regard for his devotion to the cause which he had entered in his early life. I was talking last evening with a young man, a former resident of your county, and remarking to him that among the remarkable men of our time was Christopher Layton; and that among the most remarkable body of men that had ever been brought together in this world, were the men who established themselves in these valleys in the early day. Standing upon the corner of one of the blocks of Salt Lake City, I enumerated to this young man and pointed to the homes of men who had been residents in a certain section of Salt Lake City, to the place they had taken among their fellow men, and to the characteristics and strength of the body of men whom the Almighty had selected for the accomplishment and establishment of his work. We talk about education. The world you know are making every effort that it is possible for them to make in the line of what they call the higher education; that the school may be utilized for the benefit of the human race in every possible form, and they are schooling them scientifically. It takes a scientific man to be a captain of one of our steamships. It takes a scientific man to be a master mechanic on board one of those boats. It takes a man schooled and trained in the accomplishment of those purposes looking to the naval interests of our country, to our military interests, to our civil interests, etc. Here was a man educated up to the highest possible standard, not in the scholastic training, or in the training of the schools; but in that practical common sense, that ability and force and power that from the elements right around him he has wrung a fortune, been enabled to provide for an immense household, pointing the way by which from the sordid elements the blessings of life could be wrung; all through that master education, the great common sense which the Almighty gave him. He has been a blessing to hundreds and thousands of his fellow men. Thousands of men and women among the Latter-day Saints who have come in contact with him, and been under his advice and companionship, must say if they tell the truth of him, "he was a blessing to me, he was a blessing to my home, he pointed the way in some measure to the success that has attended my life." While he possessed characteristics that I was not pleased with, his native individuality and strength and power and skill with which God had endowed him, made him a tower of strength and blessing to hundreds and thousands of his fellow men. I am not here to bestow eulogies upon Brother Layton. You knew him, you knew his characteristics. You knew the forcefulness of his nature and the faith with which God had endowed him. You knew the determination that was in him that said "there shall be no drone in the hive of our God." If there was necessity of labor or strength or power, he possessed it, and he has utilized it with the ability which his Maker has given him for the blessing of his fellow men. Under what circumstances he may have been placed, he has never betrayed

a friend; he has never betrayed the gospel of
the Lord Jesus Christ; he has never betrayed
his Redeemer; he has never betrayed his Maker
or the principles of truth so far as he had light
and knowledge and understanding to guide
and govern his life. If he has made any mistakes, they have been mistakes of the head and
not of the heart. I found fault with him upon
one occasion because of his devotion and
friendship to men that I thought were bad
men, and he regarded me as extremely harsh
in the judgment that I passed in regard to
those men. Two years later, in meeting him,
he came to me and confessed that the position
that I had assumed in regard to the matter
was correct, and that his friendship had warped
his judgment in connection with this matter,
and that he had been placed in a position that
was unfortunate from that friendship. It is
not for me to say here that he was without
fault. It is not for me to say here that there is
any man or woman or child without fault, and
to heap encomiums without wisdom or judgment upon the heroic men who laid the foundation of this commonwealth and whose hearts
were in tune with liberty, and with the determination fixed and established among them,
that every man, woman and child who accepted
a belief in the supreme Being, who desired to
do his bidding, should be blest by their coun-

sels and their efforts. This was the case with
this man who established himself here. He
returned to the southern land as one of the
saviors of the Latter-day Saints, carrying the
standard of our nation, and being one of the
means that led to the preservation of the Latter-day Saints in the midst of many of their
trials. We could point to his heroic acts, and
of his associates, who offered themselves that
the interests of our government might be extended. And returning to these fields, utilized his means in the purchase of large tracts
of country, placing it in the reach of others;
devoting himself with the energy that should
have been found in a young man of twenty
years. Almost to the day of his death was he
planning and scheming that the borders of
Zion might be extended, and that the men and
women who had come under his watch-care,
should be put upon the soil, that they might
have blessings such as the possession of homes
could give. My brothers and sisters, as I look
over the past, and as I note the changes that
are being daily wrought in the passing of that
heroic band who built up that civilization that
we possess, while a tear of regret at separation
may pass down my cheek as I note one by one
passing behind the scenes, I rejoice in the fact
that I have known them. I feel that I am a
better man for having known Christopher Lay-

ton; for having seen the liberality of his soul
and the products of that wisdom that God gave
him and the use he made of his powers. And
I might go on and point out hundreds and
thousands of them; for I bow my head in reverence to them all. Each one was a hero, no
matter where they had been placed. They had
their selfish make up; they had their peculiar
characteristics; for every one of them was distinct. This man was unlike every other man I
ever met. He was himself, Christopher Layton,
guided by a belief in God, and with a determination by the help of the Almighty, to extend the
borders of Zion, conquering the desert and
bringing to man's dominion those elements that
tend to his happiness and peace, and are a blessing to all who desire homes and a place among
the people of God. Sitting around me are
men who have drunk from the bubbling foun-
tain of truth with him, who knew his worth,
who have plighted their faith with him, pledged
their lives to him, and for whom he has pledged
his life in the accomplishment of spreading the
truth of the gospel. His talents, his means,
everything that man holds dear, was upon the
altar for the accomplishment of the work of
God. Not an apostle of the old school from
President Young down to myself, at least, but
what has received of his hospitality, been cared
for in his homes, hauled in his wagons, drank

from his wells, slept in his beds, and received
from his hand if need be the means with
which to pay our way over the railroads, or
to be carried hundreds and thousands of miles
possibly under the watchcare and protection of
his sons or the men in his employ. Not one of
them but when they come to his bier may come
from reverence, for in his death one of the tru-
est, one of the most stalwart, one of the most
fearless, most sterling of men has surrendered
his spirit to his Maker, and has gone to the reward of the just. A man who followed the
laws of God and fulfilled the purpose of his being to the best of his ability with which his
Maker had endowed him. This is my tribute.
Peace to his ashes. May his sons and daughters prove of the same worth and honor such
as was in him. May they bow at his bier and
register a vow, both sons and daughters, children and grandchildren, that that honor main-
tained by him shall never be lowered by them;
not one of them shall become a drunkard; not
one a profane man; not one a thoughtless, im-
pure or unwise man or woman; but with heroic
courage say that the standard he has raised so
high shall continue to ascend and grow in
power as long as time shall be. I regarded
President Layton as an honest, truthful, fearless believer in the principles of the gospel, and
as devoted to its advancement as any man with

whom I have come in contact in my experience with the work and its development; and it
has been my privilege to know quite a number
of them. But when we come to speak of one of
these men, and look over the past, I cast my
eye around me, look upon the men sitting by
my side, and I see that the reaper is gathering
and gleaning from a host of the worthiest men
that have ever lived in this world; and that
that gatherer will continue to come and gather;
and I wonder as I look around on their sons
and daughters, whether there is one of us who
have descended from that stalwart stock, that
will lower the standard that they raised in any
degree, and whether the sires and the mothers
who have borne us shall bow their heads in regret that they upheld the principles of the eternity of the marriage covenant and the laws of
God given for the establishment of righteousness in the world, and the gathering in of God's
children; or whether we may bow our heads
and shrink from the labor that lies before us.
I trust that such shall not be the case. We
may be weak; we may lack the capacity that
these sires have; but we can do our duty with
the ability that we have. And so far as I am
concerned, I have registered my promise with
my God, that if he will give me strength, the
mother that bore me and went to her rest in
my infancy, shall not blush that I am her son;

for I honor her that she accepted the marriage
covenant and the plurality of wives. I honor
her in the presence of God and of men, that
she sustained the principle of right. May heav-
en's peace and joy abound in the homes of
these boys and these girls, of these men and
these women, of these mothers who have passed
through the fire and trial of experience, and
been devoted and true and unyielding, fulfill-
ing their mission. May God sustain them with
that fortitude, that through the balance of their
lives they shall recognize the fact that the
Father has honored them in the possession of
such a husband; and I know that he feels that
God has honored him in the possession of such
wives and such children. The gospel, my
brothers and sisters, is true; it will not fail;
its promises will be accomplished, and the star
of light will spread and increase until all the
world shall learn the way; and the righteous
shall reign and the evil shall go to condemna-
tion. God bless you all, my brothers and sisters. May peace abide and abound in your
homes. May the heroic spirit continue to
struggle as long as breath shall remain in your
body; characterize you as it characterized this
man whose remains lie here. Not sinking your
individuality; not losing iyourself. For he
never sank his individuality. Wherever he was
his voice must be heard, giving his views upon

any proposition looking to the development in
the section in which he lived, or for the accomplishment of good. My witness is that our
Father has gathered another gem, and that he
will gather others in brief periods of time, to
link with the grand heroes that have gone before, who sustaining the name of Christ in this
world, will sustain it in the next world, as gems
adorning the crown he shall wear, because they
accepted his principles and labored to make
them honorable in the world. God bless you.
Amen.

REMARKS BY STAKE PRESIDENT JOHN W. HESS.

I feel as if I wanted to occupy a few moments. There has already been a great deal
said, and I testify, so far as my knowledge goes,
that it is all true, and not one word that I know
of has been spoken amiss. And I suppose that
we might go on and keep up this kind of talk
until dark, and we would not exhaust the good
that might be said. It is true that as a people,
when we come to a time that our hearts are
filled with charity, our hearts are filled with the
spirit of truth, so that we forget all of the little matters that once perhaps disturbed us more
or less. When we forget these little matters and
begin to think with a charitable feeling upon
one another, there seems to be no exhaust-

ing it. It is not only so in the case of Brother Layton, but it is so with the great majority of this people, as we have already heard. Now I have been acquainted with Brother Layton a great many years, and much has been said of his nobleness of character and the greatness of his intentions and desires. I want to go back. You know I am one of these old residents. I want to go back about fifty years, perhaps more. I want to go back to 1846, and I want to relate a circumstance in which this man participated, that there has been nothing said about. A circumstance that many of our young people know nothing at all about. A circumstance and a time when the Church, when the Latter-day Saints were on the altar of sacrifice, if you know what that is. These people have been on the altar of sacrifice a number of times, and the Lord has had his means at those different times to save the people. I want to relate in short, a circumstance of this kind that took place about the time of our exodus from Nauvoo. We were generally bad, so considered by the world; as a rule it was considered by the world that we were not fit to live, that we ought not to be allowed to live because we were so generally bad, and so corrupt that we were not worthy of a place on the earth. This was about the time that we were driven from Nauvoo. Now the question when we were about to be driven out of the confines of the United States was, what shall be done with these Mormons? We can't have them here; the state of Missouri couldn't endure them; they have driven them to Illinois and they have come here. We can't have them, and what are we going to do with them? Well, we were to be driven somewhere, no one knew where; into the wilderness; into the west; none of us knew where. This was a question in Congress. Now I have heard this explained in a different light, and it is simply not true wherein it has been explained in a light that it was a favor; it was a blessing conferred upon our people to allow five hundred men to enlist to go to Mexico and to be landed in California or somewhere else where we were to be going; that it was done as a matter of favor. I say it is not true. The devil did not intend such a thing; did not intend to favor us as a people; it was always the opposite; and these were the devil's emissaries scheming and planning what to do with the Mormons. Thomas Benton was a congressman from Missouri. He was figuring in Congress, and induced the President to give an exterminating order; instead of allowing the Mormons to go to the west, to be driven among the Indians, to give an exterminating order and kill the people all off. The question was asked

Benton, "what will you do with the women and
children?" "Kill them all, they are not worthy
to live, there shall not one of them be left
alive." In the character of Thomas L. Kane,
the Lord moved upon him to take a trip up
through the camps of the Saints as they were
scattered from Nauvoo to the Bluffs, and see
their condition, and if need be to do so, to go
and make a report to the President of the condition of the people, and of the innocence of
the people, and of the loyalty of the people;
that they were not disloyal to our government,
but that we had been driven from everything
that we had, and we were on the road somewhere, nobody knew where. He induced the
President to take notice of this matter. And
during this time the war with Mexico was going on, and the argument came up in Congress.
Mr. Kane said: "The people are not disloyal,
Mr. President, and to prove to you, give me
one more chance. Call upon them for five hundred of their men to go to Mexico to fight the
battles of the United States, and if they refuse
to go, I will cease importuning." The President took up with this offer and the demand
was made. Captain Allen to my certain knowledge, with five dragoons, came to us, and I
know he was the man that was sent out to recruit these five hundred men from the Mormon camps. I know that because I was there;

and to cut my story short, this call was made
upon the Mormon people to turn out five hundred of their able-bodied men, the strength, the
physical force, the strong arm of the people
was called forth, while our people were scattered from Nauvoo, from the Mississippi River to the Council Bluffs; with the people
camped along the road, and many of them all
the shelter they had was the shade of a tree.
Yes, without any support; the fathers were
called, the husbands were called, the sons were
turned out to make up these five hundred men.
What for? To go as a sacrifice. You have
many of you read of Abraham offering up
his son Isaac upon the altar. Our people at
that time, the Latter-day Saints at that time,
were as much on the altar of sacrifice as
Isaac was in the days of his father. And the
call of five hundred men was the means the
Lord used at that time as a sacrifice for Israel.
And the men were furnished, and the people
were saved, and permitted to go on their journey to the Rocky Mountains; and we are here
as we are. I see one man on the stand besides myself, and in connection with Christopher Layton and others we went as a sacrifice while Israel was on the altar. I say, my
brethren and sisters, that these things are true,
and I want to tell them for the advantage of
the young people that are here. This was one

of the efforts the evil one has made from time
to time in the history of our people to destroy
the people of God, to annihilate and destroy
every man that held the priesthood of the Son
of God, and every woman and child, that they
might be wiped out. The Lord has used men
and women from time to time to save Israel,
and this one that I refer to was used to save
Israel at that time. If these men had not been
furnished, if President Young had said, "no,
gentlemen, you have driven us from our homes,
you have robbed us of everything, and we have
been driven from everything; and now to come
and ask us to turn out our men, the strength of
Israel, when we are under such conditions, no,
gentlemen, it is too unreasonable, it is so un-
just we will not do it."   If he had done this,
there never would have been a Latter-day
Saint in these valleys, because their doom was
sealed to wipe this people from the face of the
earth.   And that was the only means that
saved them at that time. This man was one of
those who took his life in his hand. As the
angel said to Abraham when Abraham had
raised the knife, he said, "stay thy hand, Abraham, there is a ram in the thicket; sacrifice
him." These men were the ram in the thicket,
they were the sacrifice to deliver Israel; and
this man was one of them. I pray that we
may be as full of integrity as we were at that

19

time, and as many of us have been since that
time, always ready to be sacrificed for the good
of others. I ask the Lord to bless his family.
I was a great friend of Brother Layton. He
had his peculiarities, and some of them I did
not like very well. I have peculiarities that
some of you do not like very well, but I have
them all the same, and I am trying to get rid
of them; and I ask you to extend your charity towards me, and towards one another, because there is more or less good in all of us;
and with all of our weaknesses, we have no
desire, no intention to do wrong. But we have
our weaknesses, and if we had more charity
toward one another before we are dead, it
would be a blessing to us, because we would
enjoy it to some extent. May the Lord grant
it and bless this people, that they may emulate
every good example, and that they may do at
least as well as he has done, is my prayer.
Amen.

REMARKS BY PRESIDENT LORIN FARR, OGDEN.

I am pleased to meet with you, and I am
pleased to hear the words that have been spok-
en today in regard to our beloved friend Brother Layton. I have been acquainted with him
ever since he came to these valleys. I have
known his history; I have known his integ-

rity, and that his integrity has been good. I loved him because he was a man that was not afraid to speak his mind. He was not afraid to tell it, and if his mind differed from those over him, he was willing to submit to the majority, but we got his mind. I loved him for that. It is the class of man I am. I love those that are not afraid to speak their minds; and above all I like their minds to be the mind of God, the will of God, and on the side of right. The Lord God is right. And it has afforded me a great deal of pleasure in meeting here this afternoon, to witness the good feeling and the good things said in regard to Brother Layton. The last time I saw him in Arizona, I had a very pleasant time with him, stopped all night with him, and found him to be a true friend there, and I always felt blest in his society, because he was a friend of God, and God was his friend. With all his peculiarities, he was a man of integrity and tried to do right, and he has gone to his rest. He has not gone far. He is not a great ways off. We don't have a great ways to go if we have gone to a good place. President Layton has, and I am thankful that he has gained the hope and that he has got through with his troubles. He has gone to associate with holy and pure beings. I pray the Lord to bless his family and comfort them, that they may follow his good examples and seek to do all the good they can. I ask the Lord to bless you and preserve you in the truth, that you may take that course that you may meet Brother Layton again with joy and pleasure, and meet all the righteous ones that have gone before, is my prayer, in the name of Jesus. Amen.

REMARKS BY BROTHER RALPH DOUGLASS, OGDEN.

I am happy to meet with you here today. I do not want to occupy the time. I have been acquainted with Brother Layton for fifty-six years, worked with him fifty-six years ago in Illinois, and I have been acquainted with him ever since. And I know that he was a good man; and I hope we will all work so as to get salvation as he has, and that his family may do the same, and that they may have the credit that he has got. That is my prayer, in the name of Jesus. Amen.

REMARKS BY BROTHER WILLIAM C. RYDALCH, GRANTSVILLE.

My brethren and sisters, I am pleased that I have taken the opportunity to come to pay my respect to my beloved brother and friend, whom I have been acquainted with about forty-five years. And I can bear testimony that the

words that have been spoken by the brethren
are true. Whatever I have known about him
has been for good. He was a good neighbor,
a true friend, true to the Lord; gave good
counsel to his brethren ˎand sisters. I hope
and trust that we will all serve our God as
faithfully as he has, and ask my Heavenly
Father to bless the family, the sons and the
daughters, and his wives, and all who are near
and dear to him, is my prayer, in the name of
Jesus. Amen.

REMARKS BY BISHOP PETER BARTON.

I have been acquainted with Brother Layton
and the work that he has been performing, and
can bear testimony to the same. And it is a
satisfaction to the Latter-day Saints, that we
will be rewarded for the good that we have
done. None can deprive us or rob us of our
reward which is promised unto us if we are
faithful. And it should be a stimulus to each
and every one to put in practice the good examples of those that have stood the test and
that fought the good fight, and have labored so
many years in the cause of truth and to establish the kingdom of God here upon the earth.
We should try to emulate the good examples
and profit by their experience, and if we do so
we will grow up to be honored of God, and it

will be said of us when we pass away, that
we have been faithful and have labored to build
up the kingdom upon the earth; and that this
may be our part and our privilege is my prayer,
in the name of Jesus. Amen.

"O my Father, Thou that dwellest;" by the
choir.

PRAYER BY BROTHER JOHN THORNLEY.

O God our Heavenly Father, who dwellest
in the light, look down upon us thy children in
the multitude of thy tender mercies. Accept
the gratitude of our hearts for what our ears
have heard this afternoon; for the goodly portion of thy Holy Spirit which has been shed
abroad in the hearts of thy children who have
come to pay a last tribute to one of thy noble
Saints who has gone to dwell with the righteous. O Lord, do thou bless the remarks that
have been made unto us, that they may sink
deep into our hearts, that we may profit by the
same. Bless this family with the power and
the gift of the Holy Spirit. Be with them both
by day and by night, and may they prove themselves worthy of these blessings being poured
out upon them as they have been poured out
upon their parent and husband. To this end
we ask thy blessing to rest upon all in Israel
who are scattered throughout the length and

breadth of the land. Bless this people, O Lord.
We ask these mercies with all others that we
need in the name of Jesus Christ, our Redeemer. Amen.

———

After the services father's body was interred
in the Kaysville cemetery, where shortly after,
his families erected a monument.

———

PERSONAL CHARACTERISTICS.

In stature Christopher Layton was nearly
six feet in height. He had a compact and
well-knit frame; walking in an erect and state-
ly manner. His features were regular, with a
broad forehead and over-hanging eyebrows.
He had blue eyes and light hair. His expres-
sion was changeable, varying from a smile
which revealed a heart full of deep sympathy,
love and affection, to a stern, cold look, indicating strong will, self-reliance and mastery at
rebuke. He was easy and void of affectation,
deliberate in speech, conveying his original
ideas in apt though homely phraseology. He

was outspoken and plain, never mincing matters with any one, high or low, nor treating the simplest honest member of the Church with less deference than the greatest of all the distinguished men and women with whom he associated.

Without the least shadow of vanity we can truly say of him, his integrity was unimpeachable, and he was trustworthy in all the social relations and business transactions of life; and he carefully trained his children to habits of industry, economy and strict morality, and a knowledge of true religion as revealed to the prophets of the latter days.

He was a good judge of character and had an excellent memory. His mind was as capable of grasping and deciding upon great questions as of directing the smallest details of life's everyday affairs. He was a strong believer in the divine mission of Joseph Smith, and a staunch supporter of Brigham Young and his successors. His duties and responsibilities were discharged with scrupulous punctuality and that inflexibility of purpose which insures success, and from childhood he exhibited that energy and decision of character which marked his progress in life. He not only taught profound doctrine, but also how to beautify the home, how to build towns and to redeem the desert. His advice was sought for its wisdom and moderation, while he was loved for his hearty, genial soul and his deep convictions of right and justice.

When a colony was called to pioneer a new country, he was the man for the place, ready at the appointed hour. His mind was keen and far-reaching while he inherently possessed those attributes which make leaders and counselors. By hardships, trials and toil (which had been his portion) he had been tempered mentally and physically to endurance.

He had his faults, some of which were grave but not serious, but his defects need no apologies, for his virtues swallowed them up. He left a worthy example of energy, industry, indomitable will, self-sacrificing nobility, fatherly nature, love of mankind and love of God; and coming generations will link his name with the noblest characters of earth.

Christopher Layton—The Man.

MY first acquaintance with Christopher Layton dates from an evening in the sixties, when, in charge of a small train of wagons hauling grain from Cache Valley to Salt Lake City on Deseret News account, I as a boy drove into his broad dooryard at Kaysville, and found welcome entertainment for man and beast over night. The patriarchal size and character of his family, his homely, clean-cut conversation with them around the blazing fireside, his simple yet sincere devotional exercises before separating for the night—all made an impression upon me which I have never forgotten.

I met him again, as incidentally referred to in the foregoing history, in Arizona during the "crusade days" in 1885. Like many another, he was being hunted and hounded, until he scarcely knew which way to turn for safety. I encountered him on one of the flat barren deserts of that southern territory, and will not soon forget the pleasure he evinced in meeting friends when he had almost suspected and was resolutely prepared to come into clash with enemies. Patience by this time had well-nigh ceased to be a virtue with him and he chafed under the restraints and the seclusion his brethren advised. His cool, calm courage seemed to me so admirable that this meeting also made a deep impression upon me. While this "crusade" was still raging, we met again under somewhat uneasy circumstances—this time on a train between Salt Lake and Ogden —and it was my good fortune to assist him in baffling those who thought they at last surely had him in their grasp. Again he displayed the admirable resourcefulness and courage with which I had learned to associate him. I believe he never had a thought of fear; and I, like everybody else with good red blood, always admired a brave man.

The work I have bestowed upon the preceding Autobiography has but emphasized the impressions I received of him in my youth, confirmed by acquaintance with him in my maturer

years. Christopher Layton was one of the
great men of this wonderful community of
Mormons. In the group of the remarkable
ones who were the leaders in the making of
the commonwealth, he instinctively took and
held his place. Handicapped more than any
of his associates by reason of lack of school-
education, he nevertheless proved himself no
whit their inferior in judgment, wisdom, fore-
sight, energy, and the great practical qualities
that make for success. In the race, unequal
though it might have seemed, he was never left
behind; he was in every respect a worthy and
respected colleague of the biggest and brain-
iest. A natural pioneer and colonizer, he developed with years the rare high attributes of
the empire-builder; and his name will be held
in honorable remembrance as long as men shall
inhabit the great inter-mountain west.

Perhaps no man ever practiced better than he
a thorough devotion to the gospel of Work.
Tirelessly industrious himself, he felt pity, if he
did not feel contempt, for an idle person. His
life was one continued scene of active energy,
and all who approached him came perforce

within its influence. His family were taught to work, for he set them the good example; and any neighbor needing help—if he were but industrious—came to him not in vain. The list of those who credit him with giving them their start would be a long one; of worthy unfortunate to whom he turned a deaf ear there is not one.

Another trait was his intense spirituality. To expect this in a man so essentially practical as he was might seem a contradiction, for the one is usually thought to be the very antithesis of the other. Yet he was spiritual to an eminent degree. He was finely susceptible to influences which are felt by but few, and the foregoing pages contain many instances where premonitions and impressions gave him warning of events about to happen. His faith in his Maker and his confidence in His servants was great and unyielding; and he desired above all other things that this should also be the case with his posterity. He had abounding love for his family, and his children were reared in a godly atmosphere; in evidence of which it is only necessary to observe that so far as is

known at this time, every one of his numerous posterity stands in full fellowship in the
Church which their father loved and served so
well; many of them hold positions of prom-
inence and responsibility in it; and all who
have married have sought, at whatsoever ex-
pense of time, travel and money, to have the
ceremony, if not at first performed, at least
later confirmed, in sacred places. All through
his history, after his children began to grow in
years, he speaks fondly of their labors with
and assistance to him; and it was with worthy
pride that he was able to say, when in the
evening of his days, that not a single son or
daughter had ever been disobedient to him.
His word in his great household was indeed
law; but it was such because he ruled by love
and not by fear, and had won the absolute
confidence and affection of all who bore his
name.

His colonizing labors speak in their results
more eloquently of him than any historian's pen
could hope to do. His monuments are found
in numerous vast garden spots of Arizona,
where his energy and example gave him a

founder's fame; and notably in that bounteous
Utah granary—the northern part of Davis
county. He was the first to make commercially
successful the now gigantic business of dry-
farming of wheat. His Autobiography tells of
the sneers and doubts of those who watched his
initial experiment; but it does not tell an inci-
dent that is more interesting: how a well-
known miller of Salt Lake City went with mis-
giving and against his will to look at the Bishop's ripening crop, returned delighted after
contracting for it, and from that 5,000-bushel
purchase put forth a brand of flour that gave
his mill a reputation which it enjoys to this
day. Not less difficult is it to estimate the
importance of the consequences attending the
introduction of alfalfa, or lucern—an epoch-
marking experiment in which he was largely
instrumental. No one can calculate the millions of dollars in value which this great for-
age plant has secured to the inter-mountain
country during the last forty years. As a
matter of fact, the West of today without it
could not have come to pass. It has solved
graver problems, and made habitable more sec-

tions, and conferred greater benefits, than any other single element or several of the best of them combined. Before its advent, Utah and its neighboring communities had almost reached the end of their tether, so far as concerns the feeding of domestic animals. Christopher Layton's importation of seed from Australia, and its planting in Davis county, heralded the coming of a new day in western agriculture. Its success was instantaneous, and its beneficent results are limitless. To have been the pioneer in this one great enterprise alone would be of itself enough to entitle any man to grateful remembrance at the hands of posterity; and yet this is but one of many things that have made secure his place on the list of the community's benefactors.

His vivid story of experiences with the Mormon Battalion is made doubly interesting by the fact that nearly four decades later he was the leader in establishing prosperous homes and busy towns at various points along the trail of that immortal march. His recital, too, of incidents connected with the "Carson Valley mission" is a valuable contribution to history, since but little has been heretofore recorded concerning that expedition.

The effects of the perusal of this little book will be more far-reaching, I believe, than he or his family could have anticipated. He was so essentially a public character that the public are entitled to know more about him than is perhaps generally known. This autobiography lays bare the guiding motives and the impelling forces of his eventful life. While it commemorates with due modesty some of his achievements and successes, it is not silent on the trials and obstacles he was forced to meet. In its entirety it should constitute not only a joy and a comfort to his family but also an inspiration to all others who shall read it.

JNO. Q. CANNON.

Genealogical Appendix

PARENTS OF CHRISTOPHER LAYTON

SAMUEL LAYTON, born 1787, in England; died March 21, 1859, at Kaysville, Utah.

ISABELLA WHEELER, born ——, in England; died March, 1850, at Thorncut, Bedfordshire, England.

THEIR CHILDREN
(All born at Thorncut, Bedfordshire, England)

JOHN, born Aug. 7, 1815; died July 3, 1886 in Kaysville, Utah. Had son Abraham, who also came to Utah, had seven children, and died about 20 years ago; also daughter, Mary Ann (m. John Traugott) living in Davis County, Utah.

BATHSHEBA, born ——; died ——, in England. Married — DENTON; had one son, Charles, who came to Utah and accompanied his uncle to Arizona. Dead.

AMOS, born ——; died —— in childhood.

PRISCILLA, born ——, married to SAMUEL MARTIN, and died in St. Louis, U. S. A. in 1851; had five children, who all came to Utah, married and are living here still.

CHRISTOPHER, born March 8, 1821; died Aug. 7, 1898 at Kaysville, Utah.

POSTERITY OF CHRISTOPHER LAYTON

FIRST FAMILY

CHRISTOPHER LAYTON, married July 10, 1842, at Thorncut, England, by Rev. Taddy, MARY, daughter of William MATTHEWS and Elizabeth Roundy, born ——, England; died Sept. —, 1845 at Big Mound, Ill.

THEIR CHILDREN

WILLIAM, born on Atlantic ocean, Feb. 14, 1843; died March 28, 1843, on Mississippi river, near St. Louis, Mo.

ELIZABETH, born Aug. 17, 1844, at Nauvoo, Ill.; married to WILLIAM GALBRAITH, April 11, 1861, at Kaysville, Utah, by Christopher Layton; died, Feb. 13, 1908 at Raymond, Alberta, Canada.

Her Children
(All born at Kaysville, Utah)

William L., b. Jan. 12, 1862; m. (1) Ann Elizabeth Bodily, Dec. 22, 1886 (d. May 19, 1904); (2) Annie Pearl Curtis, Feb. 10, 1909.

Mary L., b. Sept. 24, 1864; m. (1) Chas. C. Hyde, March, 1883; and (2) Elijah Laycock, Nov., 1889; d. Jan. 14, 1908 at Raymond, Canada.

George, b. Nov. 6, 1866; d. Oct. 4, 1868.

Christopher, b. Feb. 28, 1869; m. Mary Heva Johnson, March 23, 1895 at Diaz, Mexico.

Peter, b. Sept. 16, 1871; d. June 4, 1873.

David, b. March 30, 1883.

SECOND FAMILY

CHRISTOPHER LAYTON married, May 3, 1850 at Sandy church, Thorncut, England, by Rev. Cook,

SARAH, daughter of John MARTIN and Mary Ann Price; born, Nov. 29, 1822 at Thorncut, England; died, Oct. 25, 1864 at Kaysville, Utah.

THEIR CHILDREN

WILLIAM, born May 1, 1851 at St. Louis; died August —, 1851 at St. Louis.

CHRISTOPHER, born Jan. 1, 1853, at Salt Lake City; married Jane E. Bodily, 'Jan. 18, 1874 in Salt Lake City, by Daniel H. Wells.

His Children
(All born in Kaysville)

Frank M., b. Sept. 1, 1876; m. Emma Diana Ellsworth, June 12, 1901, at Safford, Ariz., by Andrew Kimball.

Christopher B., b. July 6, 1878; m. Margaret B. Flint, Apr. 23, 1902, in Salt Lake City, by John R. Winder.

Lawrence, R. B., b. Nov. 14, 1880.

Maggie B., b. Aug. 7, 1882.

Mary B., b. Feb. 13, 1885; m. to Albert B. Barton by President A. H. Lund. in Salt Lake City, Jan. 25, 1911.

Delbert Edwin, b. Aug. 19, 1887; d. April 18, 1891.

Jennie B:, b. Sept. 25, 1889.

Roy Vernon, b. June 22, 1891; d. Jan. 30, 1892.

Eveline B., b. Mar. 19, 1893; d. Mar. 27, 1893.

Vernon Cecil, b. Feb. 12, 1896.

ELIZA ANN, b. May 28, 1856, on Humboldt
River, Nevada; married JOSEPH G. ALLRED,
Dec. 8, 1873 in Salt Lake City, by Daniel
H. Wells.   She died April 11, 1903 in
Arizona.

Her children
(The first four born in Kaysville, Utah)

Sarah M., b. Oct. 16, 1874; m. Alexander C. Hunt, June 11, 1901 at Thatcher, Arizona, by Andrew Kimball.

Christopher A., b. June 16, 1877; m.
Sylvia M. Faulkner, June 3, 1900 at
Thatcher, Arizona, by Andrew Kim-
ball.

Rhoda Olive, b. Oct. 2, 1879; d. at Kaysville, July 29, 1880.

Myron, b. July 6, 1881.

Gilbert, b. Oct. 19, 1884 at St. David,
Arizona; d. there Mar. 23, 1886.

Maggie Eliza, b. April 16, 1891 at
Thatcher, Arizona.

ERASTUS, born Mar. 18, 1858 at Kaysville,
Utah; died, Mar. 20, 1859 at Kaysville.

EMMA JANE, born May 29, 1860, at Kaysville; died there, July 13, 1861.

CHARLES MARTIN, born July 3, 1862, at Kaysville; married MARY ANN McMASTERS,
Sept. 20, 1883 at Salt Lake City, by Daniel H. Wells.

His Children
(The first five born in Kaysville)

Sarah Virginia, b. July 12, 1884; m. Mar-
ion Lee, Oct. 11, 1905 in Salt Lake
City, by President J. R. Winder.

Alexander, b. April 21, 1886; m. Della
Curtis, June, 1910, in Salt Lake City, by
President J. R. Winder.
Charles Martin, b. May 18, 1888.
Margaret Grace, b. Feb. 8, 1894.
Dora Joan, b. Jan. 7, 1896.
Mary Lucille, b. Mar. 25, 1899 at
Thatcher, Arizona.
Christopher Athol, b. Aug. 8, 1901 at
Thatcher, Arizona.
Owen Woodruff, b. Jan. 29, 1904 at
Thatcher, Arizona.

THIRD FAMILY.

CHRISTOPHER LAYTON married, Sept. 26, 1852 at Salt Lake City, by Brigham Young, SARAH, daughter of William BARNES and Elizabeth Jeffries, born July 6, 1836 at Sandy, Bedfordshire, England; died Sept. 13, 1906 at Kaysville, Utah.

THEIR CHILDREN

HYRUM JOHN, born Sept. 8, 1853 at Salt Lake City, Utah; married MARY LOUISA EGBERT, Dec. 8, 1873 at Salt Lake City, by Daniel H. Wells. He died Sept. 17, 1885 at Syracuse Junction, Utah.

His Children

Christopher Hyrum, b. Sept. 28, 1874 at Kaysville.

Mary Ann, b. Aug. 20, 1876 at Sunset Crossing, Arizona; d. July 3, 1889 at Kaysville.

Geneva E., b. Oct. 28, 1878 at Kaysville; m. D. M. Fisher, Aug., 1896.

Joseph Edwin, b. Oct. 26, 1880; m. Mary Ellen Allred, Feb. 3, 1909 at Ogden, by Father Cushnahan.

Sarah Crilla, b. Dec. 4, 1882 at Kaysville.

Myrtle E., b. Dec. 1, 1884; m. A. M. Gill, June, 1904, at Ogden.

MARY ANN, born Feb. 18, 1856 at Grantsville, Utah; married GEORGE SWAN, Dec. 12, 1878 at Salt Lake City, by Daniel H. Wells.

Her Children

(All born at Kaysville)

Sarah Louise, b. June 25, 1880; m. B. F. Yaunt, Nov. 14, 1906.

Agnes Ann, b. July 31, 1882.
Mary Lenore, b. Oct. 5, 1884.
George William, b. July 21, 1887.
Janet Innes, b. Dec. 10, 1889.
Darl Irene, b. Mar. 31, 1893.
Garnet Leone, b. Feb. 12, 1895.
Frank Ronald, b. Mar. 5, 1897.
Christopher MacDonald, b. Sept. 27, 1899.

EZRA WILLIAM, born July 11, 1858, at Kaysville; married MARY ELLEN COLEMERE, Jan. 10, 1878 at Salt Lake City, by Daniel H. Wells.

His Children

George Christopher, b. Oct. 7, 1878 at Kaysville; m. Annie Secrist, Nov., 1898 in Salt Lake City, by John R. Winder.
Rachel Pearl, b. Oct. 1, 1881 at Kaysville; m. Walter W. Stewart, Nov. 23, 1905 in Salt Lake City, by John R. Winder.
Sarah Mabel, b. Feb. 26, 1885 at St. David, Arizona; d. Jan. 11, 1887 at Kaysville.
Leo Hyrum, b. Mar. 24, 1891 at Kaysville.
Roy Ole, b. Nov. 10, 1896 at Kaysville.

DAVID EDWIN, born Oct. 17, 1860, at Kaysville; married ALICE WATT, Jan. 6, 1886 at Logan, Utah, by Marriner W. Merrill.

His Children

Maud, b. Sept. 30, 1886 at Kaysville; m. Jan. 11, 1911, Alfred Ryre in Salt Lake City.
Julia, b. April 8, 1888 at Kaysville.
Sarah B., b. May 3, 1890 at Kaysville.

Ziporah, b. Oct. 12, 1894 at Layton,
Utah.
Alice Marie, b. Mar. 11, 1897 at Lay-
ton.
Isabel, b. May 28, 1899 at Layton; d.
there Oct. 30, 1900.
David Christopher, b. Mar. 3, 1906 at
Layton; d. there July 8, 1910.
Stanley W., b. July 9, 1908.

ANNIE B., born Jan. 25, 1863, at Kaysville;
married SETH CHAUNCEY JONES, Aug. 25,
1884 at Logan.

Her Children

Annie Beatrice, b. Feb. 11, 1887 at
Kaysville; m. Norman Lloyd, Dec.
16, 1908 in Salt Lake City, by John R.
Winder.
Sarah Myrtle, b. Oct. 30, 1890 at
Thatcher, Arizona.
Seth Chauncey, b. Dec. 2, 1888 at
Thatcher, Arizona, and died there
Mar. 3, 1889.

SARAH ELIZABETH, born Sept. 4, 1865 at
Kaysville; married LEVI TAYLOR, Dec. 21,
1882 at Salt Lake City, by Daniel H.
Wells.

Her Children
(Both born at Kaysville)

Sarah Emmeline, b. Sept. 27, 1883; m.
to John Smith, Sept. 7, 1905.
Levi L., b. Aug. 20, 1885; m. Priscilla
Barber, Nov. 8, 1906.

FOURTH FAMILY

CHRISTOPHER LAYTON married, in December, 1854 at Salt Lake City, by Brigham Young,
ISABELLA, daughter of Richard GOLIGHTLY and Isabella Richardson, born Aug. 6, 1836 at Newcastle, England; died Dec. 15, 1877 at Kaysville, Utah.

THEIR CHILDREN

JOHN HENRY, born Dec. 6, 1855 at Salt Lake City; married HANNAH PHILLIPS, Jan. 23, 1879 at Salt Lake City, by Daniel H. Wells.

His Children
(All born at Kaysville)

Heber John, b. Sept. 20, 1879; m. Winifred Derby, Oct. 28, 1902 in Salt Lake City.
Hannah Isabel, b. April 2, 1880; d. May 3, 1880.
Delbert P., b. May 4, 1882.
Lottie Jane, b. April 1, 1884.
Chloe Louise, b. July 10, 1886; m. Thos. Jesse Harris, June 23, 1909 in Salt Lake City, by John R. Winder.
Edward P., b. Mar. 19, 1888.
Luella ⎱ twins, b. Aug. 29, 1892.
Leo   ⎰ Leo d. Sept. 4, 1892.
Leona, b. Nov. 29, 1893.
Harold Christopher, b. Aug. 19, 1895.
Richard Glenn, b. Jan. 11, 1897; d. Aug. 8, 1897.
Frankie Josephine, b. Jan. 12, 1898.
Norma Gladys, b. Sept. 29, 1900.

JACOB ALONZO, born Dec. 18, 1857 at Kaysville; married ANN McPherson, Jan. 5, 1882 in Salt Lake City, by Daniel H. Wells.

His Children

Mary Isabel, b. Sept. 22, 1882 at South Hooper, Utah; m. Fred W. Gibson, May 20, 1903 at Ogden, Utah.

Katie, b. Oct. 31, 1884 at Kaysville; m. Enoch Harris, Mar. 11, 1903 at Ogden.

Diamon McP., b. Jan. 2, 1888 at Kaysville.

David, b. Feb. 12, 1893 at Layton, Utah.

Christopher Ross, b. Mar. 28, 1898 at Layton; d. Mar. —— at Syracuse Junction.

RICHARD G., born Mar. 21, 1860 at Kaysville; married ANNIE E. HORNE, Feb. 8, 1886 at St. David, Arizona, by Bishop P. Loughgreen.

His Children

Mary Isabella H., b. Mar. 26, 1887 at St. David, Arizona; m. Lemuel R. Pace, Oct. 2, 1907 in Salt Lake Temple, by John R. Winder.

Leonora H., b. Feb. 6, 1889 at St. David, Arizona; m. Ashael Clifford, Feb. 20, 1907, by W. D. Johnson.

Richard G., b. Dec. 27, 1890 at Thatcher, Arizona.

Martha G., b. June 18, 1893 at Thatcher, Arizona.

Sophronia G., b. April 26, 1895 at Thatcher, Arizona.

Leland H., b. Feb. 22, 1898; d. Jan. 22, 1899.

Theresa H., b. May 2, 1901 at Thatcher.
Henry Marden, b. May 18, 1910 at
Thatcher.

RACHEL, born Jan. 24, 1862 at Kaysville;
married JAMES WARREN, April 1, 1880 at
Salt Lake City, by Daniel H. Wells.

Her Children

Sarah Isabel, b. Oct 30, 1880 at Kays-
ville.
David, b. Jan. 21, 1882 at Kaysville; m.
Florence Stacy Guthrie, May 23, 1906
in Salt Lake City, by John R. Winder.
Jane, b. Dec. 23, 1884 at Kaysville.
Eugene, b. June 24, 1886 at Syracuse
Junction, Utah; d. Jan. 2, 1887.
Rachel Elizabeth, b. May 4, 1889 at
Syracuse Junction; m. Leland Elliott,
June 21, 1911, by Bishop Wood, Syra-
cuse.
James, b. Mar. 24, 1890 at Kaysville; d.
Jan. 5, 1891.
Leo, b. May 21, 1895 at Syracuse Junc.
Glenn, b. Feb. 18, 1901.
Irene, b. Jan. 21, 1906.

SAMUEL, born Oct. 21, 1863 at Kaysville;
married MARY HANNAH LINFORD, June 15,
1898 at Salt Lake City.

His Child

Leland Clifford, b. Mar. 16, 1902 at
Kaysville.

LUCY ISABEL, born Nov. 7, 1865 at Kaysville;
married FRANCIS BONE, Dec. 19, 1888 at
Kaysville, by John R. Barnes.

Her Children
(All born at Layton, Utah)

Delbert Francis, b. Nov. 10, 1889.
Ethel Isabel, b. Oct. 12, 1890.
Clarence L., b. Jan. 12, 1892.
Clyde William, b. Oct. 8, 1895.
Mary Ellen, b. Mar 13, 1900.
Alberta Louise, b. Mar. 9, 1903.
Annie L., b. Oct. 11, 1906.

JANE, born April 9, 1868 at Kaysville; died
Sept. 8, 1881 at Syracuse Junction, Utah.

FIFTH FAMILY

CHRISTOPHER LAYTON married, April 12, 1856 at Salt Lake City, by Brigham Young, CAROLINE, daughter of James COOPER and Christine ——, born Sept. 26, 1836, in Yorkshire, England.

THEIR CHILDREN

SELINA, born August 15, 1857 at Carson City, Nevada; married EDWARD C. PHILLIPS, Nov. 17, 1873 at Salt Lake City, by Daniel H. Wells.

Her Children
(The first six born at Kaysville)
Jesse Charles, b. Aug. 30, 1874; m. (1) Dora Williams, Oct. 24, 1895 (she died Dec. 1, 1896) ; (2) Elizabeth Williams, May 26, 1903 in New Mexico, by Bishop Thomson.

Christopher Edward, b. July 27, 1877; d. Dec. 28, 1891 at Thatcher, Arizona.

Franklin C., b. Mar. 8, 1880; d. Aug. 14, 1881 at Kaysville.

David Dee, b. Jan. 5, 1882; m. Eliza Annetta Phillips, Dec. 30, 1903 at Thatcher, Arizona, by Andrew Kimball.

Joseph Alvin, b. July 27, 1884; m. Jennie Syrena Merrill, Sept. 23, 1907 at Thatcher, Arizona, by Andrew Kimball.

Rudger, b. Jan. 6, 1887; m. Nancy Sims, April 5, 1906 in Salt Lake City, by John R. Winder.

Horace } b. June 16, 1889 at Thatch-
Benjamin } er, Arizona; d. same day.
Alice Selina, b. Jan. 2, 1892 at Thatcher;
m. Pratt Pace, May 25, 1910 at Thatch-
er, by Andrew Kimball.
Priscilla, b. Dec. 27, 1895 at Thatcher,
Arizona.

JAMES ALBERT, born June 13, 1859 at Kaysville; married EDITH HARROD, May 27, 1886
at Kaysville, by Bishop Peter Barton.

His Children

(First two born at Kaysville, the others
at Cardston, Canada)

James Myron, b. June 30, 1887.
Cora Caroline, b. Dec. 24, 1890.
Thomas Franklin, b. April 3, 1892.
Edith Eva, b. Jan. 17, 1895.
Ida Rose, b. Jan. 17, 1898.
Virda Alice, b. Oct. 31, 1900.
Martha Priscilla, b. Aug. 12, 1903.
Afton Erzula, b. June 7, 1907.

MARTHA ALICE, born Feb. 20, 1861 at Kaysville; married JAMES T. WALKER, Mar. 4,
1877 at Salt Lake City, by Joseph F.
Smith. She died at Kaysville, Feb. 22, 1880.

Her Children

James Frederick, b. Jan. 10, 1878 at Kaysville.
Christopher John, b. Jan. 8, 1880 at Kaysville; d. Jan. 28, 1880.

HEBER C., born Dec. 8, 1862 at Kaysville;
died there Sept. 9, 1863.

JOSEPH, born July 28, 1864 at Kaysville;
married CYNTHIA FIFE, Sept. 2, 1886 at
Safford, Arizona, by Christopher Layton.
He died May 10, 1897 at Thatcher, Ariz.

His Children

Joseph Chris, b. Sept. 14, 1887 at Thatcher, Arizona; m. Lue Irene Evans, Sept. 17, 1907 at Thatcher, by Andrew Kïmball.

Glenna Selina, b. April 26, 1889 at Layton, Arizona; d. Feb. 12, 1892 at Thatcher, Arizona.

.Edna Cynthia, b. Jan. 24, 1891 at St. David, Arizona.

William Walter, b. Oct. 3, 1892 at Thatcher, Arizona.

Iretta, b. Oct. 28, 1894 at Thatcher, Arizona.

Phebe Caroline, b. Sept. 23, 1896 at Thatcher, Arizona.

CAROLINE, born April 12, 1866 at Kaysville; married JOSEPH W. HILL, Dec. 4, 1884 at Kaysville, by Bishop Peter Barton.

Her Children

(All born at Kaysville)

Martha Alice, b. May 25, 1886.

Joseph Melvin, b. May 16, 1889; m. Cora Pearl Flint, Dec. 11, 1909, by Bishop Henry H. Blood.

Leonard, b. Jan. 25, 1893.

Jenniso, b. Sept. 6, 1902.

FRANK G., born Jan. 21, 1868 at Kaysville; died there Sept. 10, 1870.

FREDERICK, born Jan. 27, 1872 at Kaysville; married BARBARA ALLEN McGUIRE, Aug. 31. 1892 at Thatcher, Arizona, by William D. Johnson.

21

His Children

Leo, b. June 7, 1893 at Thatcher, Ariz.
Esma Cynthia, b. Oct. 10, 1901 at
Thatcher, Arizona.
Irene, b. Dec. 28, 1903 at Thatcher, Ariz.

CHAUNCEY WEST, born May 7, 1874 at Salt
Lake City; married JOSIE RADDON, June 27,
1900 at Kaysville, Utah, by Bishop Peter
Barton.

His Children

James La Page, b. Feb. 10, 1901 at
Kaysville.
Chauncey Eugene, b. Sept. 20, 1903 at
Cardston, Canada.
Raddon, b. Mar. 6, 1905 at Cardston,
Canada.

HORACE, born Oct. 26, 1876 at Kaysville;
married PHEBE CORBRIDGE, Dec. 6, 1899 at
Kaysville, by Bishop David E. Layton.

His Children

Leroy, b. Oct. 17, 1900 in Alberta, Can-
ada.
Sophronia, b. Nov. 28, 1902 at Card-
ston, Canada.
Odessa, b. July 31, 1906 at Frankburg,
Alta, Canada.

BENJAMIN, born Sept. 26, 1879 at Kaysville;
married MARY AMANDA ANDERSON, Oct. 4,
1905 in Salt Lake City.

His Child

Leon, b. July 26, 1906 at Cardston, Can.

SIXTH FAMILY

CHRISTOPHER LAYTON married, Aug. 2. 1862 at Salt Lake City, by Daniel H. Wells, ROSA ANN, daughter of William HUDSON and Mary Miles; born Sept. 22, 1846 in Little Park, Yorkshire, England.

THEIR CHILDREN

GEORGE WILLARD, born Nov. 11, 1863 at Kaysville; married JANET HILL, Dec. 18, 1884 at Kaysville, by Bishop Peter Barton.

His Children
(The first five born at Kaysville, the others at Layton, Utah)
George, b. Aug. 1, 1885; d. Aug. 1, 1885.
Joseph, b. Sept. 3, 1886; d. Sept. 8, 1886.
Pearl Beatrice, b. Oct. 29, 1887.
Vera Louise, b. Oct. 20, 1891.
Cora Emmeline, b. Feb. 20, 1894.
Mamie Alta, b. Dec. 16, 1898.
Glenn Seymour, b. Aug. 22, 1900.
Leonard H., b. Nov. 6, 1902.

ALBERT THOMAS, born Dec. 28, 1865 at Kaysville; married ALMEDA MARINTHA TIBBETTS. April 7, 1887 at Layton, Arizona, by Christopher Layton.

His Children
(First five born at Layton, Arizona; the others at Franklin, Arizona)

Rose Ellen, b. Sept. 19, 1888; m. Erastus Moore, July 4, 1907 at Franklin. Arizona.

Myrtle Almeda, b. Nov. 23, 1890; m.
John Hall, May 1, 1907 at Franklin,
Arizona.
Bertha Minerva, b. Nov. 10, 1892; m.
Bartlett Gale, Aug. 31, 1910 at Frank-
lin, Arizona.
·Olive Agatha, b. Dec. 6, 1894.
Hyrum Christopher, b. May 19, 1897.
Edith Belle, b. July 31, 1899.
Albert Sylvester, b. Oct. 9, 1901.
William Neal,·b. June 23, 1904.
Walter Leo, b. Mar. 22, 1907.
Marintha Geneva, b. June 24, 1910.

HEBER CHASE, born Nov. 2, 1867 at Kays-
ville; married AGNES ALMEDA WELKER,
April 7, 1887 at Layton, Arizona, by
Christopher Layton.

His Children

(All born at Thatcher, Arizona)

Heber Lorenzo, b. Jan. 31, 1888, m.
Hulda Celestia Brundage Jan. 5, 1910,
at Layton, Arizona, by Bishop J. R.
Welker.

Agnes Ann, b. Jan. 4, 1890; m. Leo.
Romney, Apr. 11, 1911 at Thatcher,
Arizona, by Bishop James R. Welker.

Adam Leroy, b. Mar. 5, 1892.

Cordella May, b. May 4, 1894.

Delmar Christopher, b. Aug. 19, 1908;
d. Aug. 30, 1908.

ERNEST, born Aug. 25, 1869 at Kaysville;
married ADA FLINT, Mar. 9, 1898 at Salt
Lake City.

His Children
(All born at W. Layton, Utah)
Itha, b. Dec. 31, 1899.
Lela, b. July 9, 1901.
Golden F., b. June 9, 1905.

ISAAC CLARENCE, born Nov. 1, 1871 at Kaysville.

MARY ISABEL, born Feb. 2, 1874 at Kaysville; married REUBEN BARNES June 28, 1893, by Bishop Peter Barton.

Her Children

(First three born at Kaysville; others at Layton, Utah)
Leona, b. Nov. 30, 1894.
Christopher J., b. Nov. 25, 1896.
Myron Nacomio, b. Oct. 27, 1899.
Leland R., b. April 29, 1902.
Marie Ruby, b. Nov. 3, 1904.
Wilkie L. ⎱ b. April 26, 1907; Wilkie d.
Wilda L. ⎰ Sept. 19, 1907.

JEANETTA, born June 12, 1875 at Kaysville; married ERNEST ZESIGAR, ——, —— at West Layton, by Bishop David Layton.

Her Children

Leo, b. Feb. 12, 1896 at West Layton.
Ernest Lawrence, b. May 9, 1900 at Bear River.
Edith, b. Aug. 12, 1902 at Bear River.

ROZINA, born Dec. 12, 1878 at Kaysville; married JOHN H. THORNLEY, Nov. 3, 1899 at Salt Lake City, by John Woolley.

Her Children
(All born at Layton, Utah)

Irene J., b. Mar. 20, 1900.
Jesse, b. Nov. 18, 1902.
Dellas L., b. Oct. 20, 1904.
Dora L., b. Mar. 4, 1908.
Henry L., b. July 26, 1910.

OLIVE, born Feb. 24, 1881 at Kaysville; married WALTER BARLOW Jan 28, 1909 in Salt Lake City, by John R. Winder.

Her Child
Walter Layton, b. May 19, 1910.

SEVENTH FAMILY

CHRISTOPHER LAYTON married, January 7, 1865, in Salt Lake City, by Heber C. Kimball, SEPTIMA, daughter of George SIMMS and Caroline Gill; born July 20, 1848 at Cheltenham, Gloucestershire, England; died Oct. 5, 1889 at Kaysville.

THEIR CHILDREN

AMY C., born Dec. 24, 1867 at Kaysville; married REUBEN WALTER FULLER, Jan. 1, 1886 at St. David, Arizona, by Bishop Peter Loughgreen.

Her Children
(Born at Thatcher, Arizona)

Maggie Drucilla, b. Nov. 21, 1887; m. Warren Bingham, Sept. 24, 1906 at Layton, Arizona, by Bishop J. W. Welker.
Reuben Walter, b. Feb. 13, 1890; m. Anna Taylor, July 23, 1908 at Pima, Arizona, by Bishop P. C. Merrill.
Lawrence, b. Mar. 21, 1894.
Archie Joseph, b. May 12, 1898.

PRISCILLA MAY, born Jan. 19, 1870 at Kaysville; married THOMAS FLITTON, Feb. 19, 1889 at Kaysville, by John R. Barnes.

Her Children

Jennie L., b. Dec. 25, 1889 at Kaysville.
Rupert Thomas, b. Oct. 21, 1891 at Kaysville.

Daniel David, b. Oct. 7, 1893 at Hooper, Utah.

Joseph Christopher, b. Nov. 3, 1895 at Kaysville.

Harry Wilford, b. Nov. 25, 1897 at Kaysville.

Curtis Monroe, b. Mar. 8, 1900 at Ogden.

Alfred Hannon, b. Sept. 26, 1902 at Syracuse, Utah.

Elmira, b. June 9, 1907 at Syracuse, Utah.

Louise } b. Oct. 11, 1909.
Louie

DRUCILLA GRACE, born Mar. 23, 1872 at Kaysville; married JOHN H. BLOOD, Jan 7, 1890 in Logan, by M. W. Merrill.

Her Children
(All born in Kaysville)

Septima L., b. Mar. 11, 1891.
Annie L., b. Feb. 24, 1894.
Merlin John, b. Aug. 3, 1896; d. July 22, 1909.
Byron L., b. Oct. 7, 1898.
Vera Jane, b. Mar. 7, 1901.
Millie L., b. Sept. 10, 1903.
Seth L., b. Aug. 6, 1905.
Nora L., b. Sept. 25, 1908.
Howard, b. Feb. 11, 1911.

OSCAR GEORGE, born May 12, 1874 at Kaysville; married LULA JANE LEWIS, May 24, 1892 at Thatcher, Arizona, by W. D. Johnson.

His Children
(All born in Thatcher, Arizona)
Blanche Septima, b. May 11, 1893.
Oscar Clyde, b. Aug. 26, 1894.
Delbert George, b. May 22, 1896; d.
Aug. 2, 1897.
Flossie, b. Mar. 2, 1898.
Bertha, b. Feb. 19, 1900.
Marlin Bruce, b. Mar. 18, 1903.
Beatrice, b. Sept. 8, 1904.
Junius Lewis, b. Mar. 15, 1906.
Jessie, b. Oct. 31, 1907.
Roy Lewis, b. Aug. 7, 1904.

HARRY WILFORD, born Oct. 7, 1876 at Kaysville; married EMILY REAY, Nov. 15, 1898 at Thatcher, Arizona, by W. D. Johnson.

His Children
(All except first one born at Central,
Arizona)
Miles Merlin, b. Sept. 7, 1899 at Thatcher.
Ralph Ray, b. June 5, 1901.
George Spencer, b. Feb. 27, 1903.
Nola Drucilla, b. Dec. 1, 1904.
Martha Opal, b. Dec. 11, 1906.
Roy W., b. Jan. 27, 1909.

FRANKLIN SIMMS, born Mar. 21, 1879 at Kaysville; died there Sept. 27, 1879.

JESSE MONROE, born Dec. 27, 1884 at Eden, Arizona; married MURIEL RANDALL (born Dec. 4, 1889, at Nephi, Utah) April 1, 1909 at Solomonville, Arizona, by Judge F. S. Bunch.

His Child
Daughter born Feb. 18, 1910; died same day.

EIGHTH FAMILY.

CHRISTOPHER LAYTON married, May 1, 1870 in Salt Lake City, by Daniel H. Wells, MARY JANE, daughter of Levi ROBERTS and Harriet Ann Neff.

THEIR CHILDREN

FLORENCE, born Aug. 3, 1871 at Kaysville; married ALBERT K. GREEN, Mar. 8, 1893 at Kaysville.

Her Children
(All born at Kaysville)

Otha K., b. Dec. 26, 1893.
Levi B., b. Sept. 27, 1896; d. April 26, 1899.
Parnell, b. Sept. 20, 1898.
Ortensa, b. Nov. 26, 1901.
Austher L., b. Oct. 4, 1903.
Mary L., b. Oct. 30, 1909.

ELLA, born Oct. 8, 1873 at Kaysville; married EDWIN WEBB, Feb. 28, 1893 at Kaysville, by Bishop Peter Barton.

Her Children
(All except first one were born at Malad, Idaho)

Earl, b. Nov. 24, 1894 at Kaysville.
Josie Mary, b. Nov. 20, 1896.
Christopher, b. May 1, 1899.
Leland, b. Oct. 2, 1901.
Verma, b. April 11, 1904.
Edmund L., b. Jan. 27, 1906.
Charles L., b. ——, ——.

LEVI BRIGHAM, born Dec. 28, 1875 at Kaysville; died Nov. 13, 1895 in Idaho.

HARRIET ANN, born Dec. 28, 1877 at Kaysville; married E. CONRAD MILLER, Dec. 9,
1893 at Salt Lake City, by Bishop Adam
Spiers.

Her Children
(All born at Layton, Utah)
Marie, b. Oct. 9, 1894.
Davina, b. April 7, 1898.
Lovina, b. April 7, 1900.
Harriet Edwina, b. Oct. 9, 1903.
Benjamin L., b. Nov. 28, 1907.
Harmon L., b. June 12, 1910.

PHEBE, born July 2, 1881 at Kaysville; married WILLARD R. HARRIS, Jan. 30, 1901 in
Salt Lake City, by John R. Winder.

Her Children
(All born at East Layton, Utah)
Leora, b. Jan. 11, 1902.
Mary Neve, b. Aug. 2, 1903.
Wayne L., b. Mar. 6, 1905.

JENNIE M., born at Kaysville Aug. 30, 1886;
married ALONZO J. GILERT, Oct. 30, 1907,
in Salt Lake City, by John R. Winder.

NINTH FAMILY

CHRISTOPHER LAYTON married, Aug. 15,
1878 at, Salt Lake City, by Joseph F. Smith,
ELIZABETH, daughter of Ebenezer WIL-
LIAMS and Ada Evans.

THEIR CHILDREN

LAWRENCE W., b. Aug. 4, 1879 at Kaysville;
died there Aug. 28, 1879.

LOTTIE W., born Nov. 18, 1880 at Kaysville;
married JOSEPH HEBER LARSON, May 25,
1903 at Thatcher, Arizona, by Andrew
Kimball.

Her Children

(All born at Thatcher, Arizona)

Magdaline, b. May 3, 1904; d. May 22,
1905.

Thora, b. Aug. 27, 1905.

Joseph L., b. Oct. 23, 1907.

LESLIE W., born Jan. 5, 1883 at Kaysville;
married NELLIE CLARIDGE, Sept. 3, 1903 at
Thatcher, Arizona, by Patriarch Samuel
Claridge.

His Children

Christopher, b. April 19, 1904 at Thatcher; d. May 29, 1905.

Angeline, b. Jan. 21, 1906 at Thatcher.

Elizabeth, b. May 30, 1907 at Thatcher.

Leslie Joy, b. Feb. 16, 1909 at Brice,
Arizona.

LILLIAN W., (twin) born Feb. 12, 1885 at St. David, Arizona; married EDWARD M. CLARIDGE, Sept. 3, 1903 at Thatcher, Arizona, by Patriarch Samuel Claridge.

Her Children
(All born at Thatcher)
Luella, b. April 5, 1904; d. May 21, 1905.
Samuel Lynton, b. Mar. 2, 1906.
Ethna, b. Nov. 19, 1908.

LUELLA W., (twin) born Feb. 12, 1885 at St. David, Arizona; married OUSLEY A. RENEER, Sept. 4, 1904 at Thatcher, Arizona, by Bishop Moody.

Her Children
(Born at Thatcher, Arizona)
Leman A., b. Oct. 8, 1905.
Ebon, b. Jan. 22, 1908.

PRISCILLA W., born Nov. 11, 1887 at Thatcher, Arizona.

MINNIE W., born Jan. 3, 1890 at Thatcher, Arizona.

GILBERT W., born April 11, 1892 at Thatcher, Arizona.

ELIZABETH W., born May 19, 1894 at Thatcher, Arizona.

WILMUTH W., born Sept. 4, 1896 at Thatcher, Arizona.

LaVergne, TN USA
31 August 2010
195273LV00007B/35/A